Advances in Contemporary Educational Thought Series

Jonas F. Soltis, Editor

D0145687

Reframing Educational Policy

DEMOCRACY, COMMUNITY, AND THE INDIVIDUAL

Joseph Kahne

Teachers College, Columbia University
New York and London

Published by Teachers College Press, 1234 Amsterdam Avenue, New York, NY 10027

Library of Congress Cataloging-in-Publication Data

Kahne, Joseph.
    Reframing educational policy : democracy, community, and the individual / Joseph Kahne.
        p.   cm.—(Advances in contemporary educational thought series ; v. 16)
    Includes bibliographical references and index.
    ISBN 0-8077-3493-4 (cloth : alk. paper).—ISBN 0-8077-3492-6 (pbk. : alk. paper)
        1. Education—United States—Philosophy.   2. School management and organization—United States—Philosophy.   3. Politics and education—United States.   4. Progressive education—United States—Evaluation.   5. Communitarianism—United States.   6. Education, Humanistic—United States.   I. Title.   II. Series.
    LA217.2.K35   1996
    370'.1—dc20   95-42598
                                                                                                            CIP

ISBN 0-8077-3492-6 (paper)
ISBN 0-8077-3493-4 (cloth)

Printed on acid-free paper
Manufactured in the United States of America
03 02 01 00 99 98 97 96 8 7 6 5 4 3 2 1

For Mom and Dad with love

As for ideals, all agree that we want the good life, and that the good life involves freedom and a taste that is trained to appreciate the honorable, the true and the beautiful. But as long as we limit ourselves to generalities, the phrases that express ideals may be transferred from conservative to radical or vice versa, and nobody will be the wiser. For, without analysis, they do not descend into the actual scene nor concern themselves with the generative conditions of realization of ideals.

—John Dewey, *Individualism Old and New*

Contents

Foreword

This is a book about the culture of policy making and about alternative purposes for education. Like all cultures, that of the policy maker and policy consumer tacitly defines the limits and boundaries of policy possibilities. The language, norms, and values of a particular conceptual, political, and ethical world view legitimate certain policy options and obscure or even constrain consideration of others.

In this book, Joseph Kahne clearly and richly describes four political and ethical postures toward policy making, policy analysis, and policy implementation: the utilitarian, the rights based, the communitarian, and the humanist. Each is grounded in a different vision of a purpose for educating people. The utilitarian sees education as serving the greatest good for the greatest number. That good is most often assessed in terms of efficiency, productivity, and the economic well-being of society. The rights-based policy maker, on the other hand, wants education to secure the legitimate rights of each individual in a democracy, stressing equality of educational opportunity and equity of access to a just share of available social goods. Kahne argues that these two frameworks dominate and define much of contemporary policy making in America.

He also argues that two extant but nonmainstream alternative frameworks, democratic communitarianism and humanistic psychology, can provide a wider and perhaps more desirable vision of the purpose of education in our society. Adopting either of these frameworks would lead policy makers to ask very different questions about what we ought to be doing to reform, improve, and assess education in the United States. The communitarian sees education's main task as developing citizens who share a commitment to democracy and to one another, respect diversity, participate in civic activities, and take part in informed debates on public issues. The humanist, on the other hand, views the growth and development of the unique talents and potential of each individual to be the highest purpose of education in a democracy and the best way to serve the common good.

Kahne uses these frameworks to great advantage when he examines two persistent contemporary policy issues, tracking and school choice, through the lens of each framework. His discussion makes it clear that one point of view can raise questions and suggest sensible answers that from another point of view would never be considered.

Recognizing the difficulty of bridging the abstract world of theoretical frameworks and the real, complex, practical, and sometimes intractable world of policy making, Kahne speaks thoughtfully about problems and possibilities to those who would like to try to do so. He also revisits the Eight-Year Study that took place between 1933 and 1941. His analysis is a fascinating reexamination of this unprecedented major longitudinal research program, whose purpose was to try to free the secondary schools from the dominance of colleges on their curricula. Through that reexamination, Kahne shows that alternative purposes, policies, and programs are possible in the real world and that our history demonstrates both professional and public large-scale support for communitarian and humanistic aims of education.

This is a book with many facets. It puts policy making and analysis in a political and ethical framework that forces one to raise serious and deep questions about what purposes our schools should serve. It offers attractive alternative visions without necessarily making them mutually exclusive but clearly asking one to choose. It provides a needed philosophical and historical perspective on ideas that tacitly underwrite many of our current policy debates. It provides great insight into the rhetoric and logic of contemporary policy making. And finally, it has the range and power to speak to a wide audience of students, scholars, policy makers, school people, and politicians, and to a concerned public. It is the kind of book that belongs in this series.

Jonas F. Soltis
Series Editor

Preface

As a graduate student I was a teaching assistant for a course called Decision Analysis. This course aimed to develop students' ability to use quantitative research when making decisions about educational policy and practice. Much of the course focused on production function studies, which assess the impact of educational inputs on particular outputs.

One day, while I was teaching the class, a student questioned the value of a research finding because the output variable was students' achievement test scores and, as she put it, "We all know that those scores are meaningless." As the class discussed this comment it became clear that many students agreed. Their concern was not simply that standardized achievement tests often have racial, gender, or class biases, but also that these tests are poor proxies for a quality education. Intrigued by their comments, I asked the class to take a minute and write down their conception of a quality education. Students were uneasy. One student asked, "You want us to write about what we really think matters—from the heart?" Since they were writing from the heart, I agreed to give them 5 minutes.

As time passed it became clear that few students had written much and that they did not feel like sharing their ideas. Rather than asking for and evaluating differing conceptions of the aims of education, we discussed the question itself. Although it was the spring quarter, none said that they had been asked to specify or reflect on the purpose of education in any of their courses.

These students were part of the Administration and Policy program. What does it mean, we asked, that students of educational administration and policy can do "high-quality" coursework without having formulated a coherent understanding of the goals that drive their endeavor?

This book is, in many respects, an attempt to write in about 200 pages what I asked the students in Decision Analysis to write in 5 minutes. I have tried to provide a framework that permits policy analysts to think about the aims of education, to weigh the pros and cons of moving in different directions, and to consider the educational and societal implications of different political and moral commitments. I also have tried to expose the orientation of those involved in mainstream policy discussions and to highlight the ways in which a commitment to two alternative perspectives might alter the form, focus, and content of policy analysis and evaluation.

Acknowledgments

When people care about their written work, they talk about it a lot—at least I did. I'm enormously grateful to those who listened, responded, and kept me going.

My parents were the most important. My goals have been shaped by their beliefs and by their example. My efforts to reach these goals are nurtured by their love, wisdom, sensitivity, and integrity. Tamar Dorfman's support was also essential. She could simultaneously care deeply about these issues while remembering that they weren't that important. This balance helped keep me sane. I'm inspired by her dedication to her students. I treasure our relationship.

I owe special debts to numerous colleagues and mentors. Bill Ayers, Larry Cuban, Julie Duff, Paul Goren, David Hansen, Rebekah Levin, Milbrey McLaughlin, Nel Noddings, Susan Moller Okin, Dan Perlstein, John Rogers, Suzanne Shanahan, Mark Smylie, Bill Tobin, Steve Tozer, and Joel Westheimer helped structure my thinking on these issues and their relationship to broader policy concerns. At the same time, they provided valued friendship, thoughtful feedback, and much needed distractions. In a variety of ways, these people told me what to write, when to write, that I was right, and that I better rewrite. I am enormously grateful.

1

The Constraining Culture of Educational Policy Analysis

Should every school lunch have a candy bar? Does the good taste of candy outweigh the nutritional problems associated with sugar?

These aren't questions policy makers commonly ask. Analyses of lunch programs tend to focus on three issues: their impact on student nutrition, the impact of lunch consumption on demand for particular agricultural products, and the impact of hunger (or the lack thereof) on test scores (see Sautter, 1978). Taste, as an end in and of itself, has not been a concern of congressional studies or policy analysts' commentaries.

Students eat roughly 2,000 school lunches prior to graduation from high school. The government spends several billion dollars each year providing meals to millions of children, and no one systematically studies the way these meals taste. Still, you ask, so what?

The failure of analysts to value the way that food tastes as an end and not a means highlights a concern that extends far beyond school lunch policy. Some worthwhile policy goals receive systematic attention from educational policy analysts, while others do not. What types of educational goals and rhetoric concerning goals are a legitimate part of mainstream policy analysis? What social and ethical priorities do these goals and rhetoric reflect? This study considers the social and ethical orientations that structure mainstream policy dialogues and the ways adoption of some alternative social and ethical priorities would change the form and focus of policy debates.

Increasingly, scholars are recognizing the value of studying "policy" as a system or a culture. Rather than focusing on particular policy issues or documents, they are examining the norms and values of the policy process and their implications for the structure and content of policy discussions (Swidler, 1982; Majone, 1980, 1989; Weiss, 1980; Bell, 1985; Fiala and Lanford, 1987; Lindblom and Cohen, 1979; Gusfield, 1981). By looking at policy analysis and discourse through the lenses of some prominent ethical and political theories, we can gain access to

1

important aspects of the policy process. This approach provides a unique perspective from which to consider both the culture of educational policy discussions and the purposes of education.

THE PROBLEM: TECHNOCRATIC TUNNEL VISION

Rather than defining and debating particular goals, educational policy makers tend to focus on the technical issues surrounding educational practice. That is, policy analysts and evaluators tend to explore varied means of efficiently and equitably pursuing an array of educational goals. They less frequently debate the desirability of these goals or the way different educational goals and processes shape individuals and society (Graham, 1984; Hacker, 1984; Newmann and Oliver, 1967; Silberman, 1971; Oakes and Sirotnik, 1983). For example, when reviewing the outpouring of extremely influential commentaries on education that appeared in the early 1980s, including the National Commission for Excellence in Education's report *A Nation at Risk*, John Goodlad's *A Place Called School*, Theodore Sizer's *Horace's Compromise*, Ernest Boyer's *High School: A Report on Secondary Education in America*, and Coleman, Hoffer, and Kilgore's *High School Achievement: Public, Catholic, and Private Schools Compared*, Andrew Hacker (1984) concluded:

> We no longer have commanding figures like John Dewey and Robert Hutchins, who, in their different ways, tried to create a vision of an educated citizenry whose members would have some chance at something that could be called the good life. That this goal, however nebulous, is all but absent from current books and reports is far more disconcerting than our lag in teaching algorithms to restless teenagers. (40).

This was not always the case. When one considers such classics as Plato's *Republic*, Rousseau's *Émile*, and Dewey's *Democracy and Education*, it becomes clear that the underlying purpose of education has been of central importance for the range of educational visions that have appeared throughout the history of Western educational thought.

Policy analysts' current hesitancy to focus on the implications and desirability of varied aims of education is problematic. One cannot judge a policy's potential to improve society without knowing both the educational goals being pursued and the alignment of these goals with the policy maker's societal goals. In other words, in addition to assessing a policy's potential effects on test scores, graduation rates, or some other educational goal, one must assess whether achieving that goal will promote a given conception of the good society.

FOUR ALTERNATIVE PERSPECTIVES

The range of social doctrines put forward by ethical and political philosophers offers one way of making meaningful connections between educational goals and societal goals. In Chapters 2, 3, and 4 I outline the societal goals associated with the political and ethical theories of utility, rights-based justice, democratic community, and psychological humanism. I also describe the analytic logic associated with each theory and describe the form educational policy discussions might take were they guided by attention to these theories.

The Mainstream: Utilitarian and Rights-Based Theories

Utilitarian and rights-based theories are the ethical foundation of our liberal democracy. They are the central ethical rationales for our economic, social, and political systems. Not surprisingly, they constitute the backdrop for mainstream educational policy discussions. In addition, whether focusing on utility or rights-based conceptions of justice, educational policy analysts commonly characterize the product of education in terms of human capital development. These priorities are reflected in the emphasis on equity, efficiency, and excellence and in arguments that stress the relation among education, productivity, and equality of opportunity.

The Critique and the Expansion: Democratic Communitarian and Humanistic Theories

Three concerns prompt my focus on democratic communitarian and humanistic alternatives to mainstream perspectives. First, democratic communitarian thought and humanistic psychology offer powerful critiques of the dominant emphasis on utility and rights. Second, the role played by education within these social and psychological theories of the good life and the good society is substantial. Finally, although these alternative perspectives get little attention from mainstream policy analysts, both sets of ethical priorities would pass what was once described to me as the "Aunt Emma" test. That is, both perspectives would strike an educator's mythical aunt as respectable. Members of the policy community might be uncomfortable evaluating a major policy initiative by focusing primarily on self-actualization or on the creation of a democratic community, but discussions regarding the fulfillment of students' full potential or of their developing democratic character would not be out of place at a PTA meeting.

Despite this popular support, these goals commonly receive only vague reference in the introductions and conclusions of policy documents. They rarely receive systematic attention from policy analysts. This neglect is both troubling and consequential. Inattention to these alternative perspectives obscures important visions of the good society and the implications of these perspectives for educational policy. This limits the scope of reflective debate and thus constrains the democratic process.

To highlight the impact of this silence, Chapters 3 and 4 examine the implications for education of positions put forward by theorists who describe alternatives to utilitarian and rights-oriented ethical systems. How, for example, should analysts design testing policies and interpret test results? Should tests be taken by individuals, or should groups of students work on a test together? Should the development of academic competencies remain the primary focus of examinations or, for that matter, of educational institutions? Considering nonmainstream political and ethical theories such as democratic communitarianism and psychological humanism highlights a host of questions that analysts might otherwise never ask.

Chapters 5 and 6 portray the ramifications of this neglect in a more concrete fashion, examining two prominent policy debates with profound implications for the organization and practice of schooling: tracking and school choice. These issues both command substantial attention and focus explicitly on the ends of education. Mapping the concerns raised in these policy discussions into the typology of educational aims discussed in Chapters 2, 3, and 4 demonstrates the degree to which mainstream policy talk is animated by a utilitarian and rights focus on human capital development. I suggest what might be added to these debates if attention were given to some alternative social doctrines.

Why are the values embodied in these alternative doctrines rarely given primacy in mainstream policy rhetoric? Many bemoan the technical focus of educational policy analysis (Oakes and Sirotnik, 1983; Majone, 1989; Scheffler, 1984). Why, then, is the focus of analysis so often on technique instead of on normative questions surrounding goals? How is it that the dominance of equity and excellence in policy discussions is so rarely questioned by policy analysts? What are the costs of "the end of ideology" (Bell, 1960) in educational policy debates?

I examine these questions by exploring the reactions of mainstream policy analysts to a major effort by prominent educators and
educational researchers to alter the ethical orientation of policy analysis and practice. In Chapter 7, I discuss the work done in the 1930s and
early 1940s by the Progressive Education Association's Commission on
the Relation of School and College. During the Commission's Eight-
Year Study, teachers, administrators, and curriculum specialists
worked in 30 schools pursuing democratic communitarian and humanistic goals. In addition, a team of evaluators carefully studied the
effects of these schools on students' development in high school and
on their performance in college. They looked both at mainstream measures of academic achievement and at nontraditional concerns such
as healthy personal development and the development of democratic
character. Records of this study provide valuable insight into some
of the implications of these perspectives for both policy analysts and
educators—and examination of mainstream responses to this effort at
reform helps to clarify some of the barriers facing reformers who endorse this alternative agenda.

THE THEORY-POLICY INTERFACE: LIMITATIONS AND ADVANTAGES

The Ragged Seams

Readers might worry that the structure of my argument minimizes
important differences between the tasks facing political theorists and
those facing policy analysts. Modern ethical theorists and political philosophers often work to develop a set of coherent principles that provide a foundation for designing social systems and considering various policy options. Utilitarian, libertarian, communitarian, and other
social theories define distinct visions of the good society, rely on different justifications, and lead their adherents to think about public policy
in dramatically different ways.

With good reason, policy analysts and activists do not orient their
analysis in this way. Instead, they adopt what Kohlberg and Mayer
(1972) term "the bag of virtues" approach. Rather than specifying a set
of educational objectives derived from a philosophy of education,
most analysts appeal to a broad array of desirable ends. They argue
that schools should promote progress, equality, good citizens, good
workers, self-esteem, critical thinkers, and well-rounded individuals.
Although this may help policy analysts balance competing moral, empirical, and political claims, there is little evidence that policy makers

can pursue all of these goals simultaneously or even agree on the meaning of these varied terms. As a result, they often sound like politicians arguing that it is time to branch out and get back to our roots. For example, educational policy makers state that schools must promote traditional community values *and* that families, not schools, are responsible for students' moral development. They write that students must be trained to participate productively in our economy *and* helped to develop freely, in accordance with their own inclinations and interests. They proclaim that we must make sure that "gifted and talented" students achieve their full academic potential, at the same time that they argue for redoubling our commitment to equality.

In addition, the kind of abstract and theoretical precision achieved by ethical and political philosophy often fails to provide public policy makers with clear direction. Two analysts whose work reflects the same vision of the good society can easily arrive at differing conclusions. Utilitarians do not all agree, for example, on the desirability of vocational education. At the same time, those who follow different political philosophies frequently recommend a similar response to a particular policy issue. For example, adherents to many differing social theories would be likely to support a policy aimed at promoting a school environment in which participants treated each other with decency and respect.

Moreover, in order to formulate decision rules for policies that rest on sturdy foundations and that align with well-developed and distinct ethical systems, ethical and political philosophers often assume away much of the complexity of political life. Rather than starting from scratch and designing the "most just" or "most efficient" funding policy, curriculum requirements, or governance arrangements, policy makers commonly begin with the standard operating procedures and ask what changes are possible in the given policy environment. They strive for incremental progress rather than perfection, and the compromises that result frequently prevent consistent adherence to a given ethical perspective. Analytic structures proposed by political, philosophical, and ethical theorists rarely order the behavior of actors in the policy arena (Wildavsky, 1987; Majone, 1989).

Enriching the Discourse

If the policy world is unavoidably chaotic and if doctrinal consistency rarely drives policy analysis, one might argue that it makes little sense to apply philosophically grounded frameworks. I may be looking through a lens and using quite different criteria than those used by the actors whose behavior I am studying. Given these concessions, is the effort to examine educational policy discussions in terms of ethical and political theories misconceived? No. Why not?

Hesitancy on the part of ethical and political theorists to compromise and endorse multiple and conflicting stances does limit the extent to which much modern ethical and political theory can be applied to current policy discussions. However, the neglect of philosophical concerns by mainstream educational policy analysts is equally troubling. At the same time that social theorists fail to develop a vision that appreciates the compromised and inconsistent nature of the policy world, most policy analysts behave as though consensus regarding the ends of education has been achieved. They fail to examine the consistency of their attempts to reform the organization and practice of schooling with various conceptions of the good society. As Patricia Graham (1984) writes:

> The late twentieth-century analogue to the history or philosophy of education became policy studies. Here the emphasis was upon analysis, a systematic and careful look at what the policy was and what its effects were. Few such rigorous analysts believed their task extended to considering what the purposes underlying the policy ought to be. (35)

Systematic attention to philosophical ideas relating educational policy to concern for the good life and the good society is essential for two reasons. First, this discussion can help analysts reflect on the policy process. More specifically, examination of the consistency of policy discussions with varied social theories can help analysts evaluate the norms and pressures of the policy process and their impact on the ethical priorities and social goals attended to by policy analysts and policy makers. The lenses offered by political theorists also enable assessment of the degree to which particular policies and types of policies can simultaneously satisfy the concerns of those with differing ideological loyalties. In addition, analysis of the rhetoric surrounding specific policy issues can focus attention on the rhetoric that legitimizes various perspectives and values. Such analysis can expose the forces shaping, constraining, and organizing mainstream rhetorics and, by inference, the broader culture.

Second, this project may help policy analysts and policy makers reflect on and critique their own educational philosophy and the desirability of various policy options. These deeply considered theories provide a language and highly developed machinery well suited for articulation and assessment of the implications and trade-offs associated with our current commitments. Although I do not believe alignment of a policy with a particular political philosophy constitutes a sufficient guide for policy analysts, I do believe that participants in the policy process have much to gain from considering these perspectives. Each of the doctrines I discuss covers a set of values that has had a secure place in Western culture. That policy analysts often act without consciously pausing to consider these perspectives does not imply that their evaluation of particular policies and practices might not change were they to engage in such a process. Mapping the implications of varied political theories onto discussions of educational policy may help those less familiar with these political theories to reflect on aspects of their own educational philosophy.

Indeed, it seems that the continuation of many practices in education results not from a conscious decision but from passive acceptance of various long-established norms. Those interested in reforming school organization and educational practice frequently point to this problem and argue that practitioners and policy makers need to reassess many of the structures and practices that characterize modern schooling. Structured consideration of the educational implications of varied ethical and political philosophies is particularly well suited to promote such critiques because it prompts analysts to clarify the values that guide their thought. Oakes and Sirotnik (1983) stress the importance of such considerations:

> If these almost universal practices [norm-referenced testing, curriculum tracking, and competitive classroom reward structures] were to be the focus of discourse, wherein their histories and underlying assumptions were revealed, the kind of social reality they imply made explicit (e.g., the nature of man, society, and education), and the consequences for individuals and society that follow from their use uncovered, it is likely that they would emerge as being in conflict with educators' conceptions of humane and democratic schooling. (21–22)

Inattention to the implications of social, political, and ethical doctrines leads to silences that obscure both desirable options and important normative issues. By focusing attention on the educational goals of a given policy and on the kinds of societal goals such educational goals imply, this framework helps policy analysts see contradictions between policies and professed values. It makes problematic commonly accepted educational goals and practices. Moreover, this framework helps explicate the policy potential of differing value orientations, including democratic communitarian and humanistic values, making it possible to imagine new policies and policy rationales.

2
Utilitarian and Rights Theory

Equity, efficiency, and excellence—these are the central concerns of educational policy analysts. In policy discussions, a commitment to efficiency is taken for granted. Substantial debates take place, however, between those who emphasize equity and those who want priority placed on excellence. Some argue that the federal government's "emphasis on promoting equality of opportunity in the public schools has meant a slighting of its commitment to educational quality [excellence]" (Twentieth Century Fund, 1983, 6). Similarly, Chester Finn (1987) writes that by focusing on dropouts we are "slowing the excellence movement" (18).

Others argue just the opposite. "The idea of educational equity has fallen from favor," writes Jeannie Oakes (1986a), "and the public have turned their attention instead to . . . excellence" (12). Finally, many write that this is a false distinction—that no system can be truly excellent without also being equitable. "What is needed," writes Michael Kirst (1984), "is a policy that fights for both goals—excellence and equity—while balancing the claims of each" (17).

This chapter will not resolve these disputes but it will discuss some important distinctions. Below I examine the utilitarian and rights-oriented philosophical theories that provide the ethical grounding for commitments to these apparently competing ideals. I also discuss the implications of these philosophical theories for those engaged in educational policy dialogues.

UTILITARIAN THOUGHT

> It is the greatest happiness of the greatest number that is the measure
> of right and wrong. (Bentham, [1776] 1969, 45)

In a single sentence Jeremy Bentham described a moral theory, a theory that seems as conceptually straightforward as it is intuitively appealing. Building on the work of David Hume, Adam Smith, the 18th-century Dutch-born philosopher Bernard de Mandeville, and others, Bentham articulated a moral and political philosophy that has shaped policy discussions and legislative goals for more than a century. His basic argument, that laws and social institutions should be designed to promote pleasure and reduce pain, still has a kind of self-evident flavor—at least within Western culture.

Many political philosophers and social theorists, however, have not been convinced. As Mary Peter Mack (1969) demonstrates, "Bentham has long since been hurled to the pit of abuse, and there he now remains" (viii). Marx, for example, called Bentham "the arch-philistine . . . the insipid leather-tongued oracle of the commonplace bourgeois intelligence . . . a genius in the way of bourgeois stupidity"; Emerson described utilitarianism as "a stinking philosophy"; and John Maynard Keynes believed that Bentham's ideas were "the worm which has been gnawing at the insides of modern civilization and is responsible for its present moral decay" (see Mack, 1963, 2).

These critics have not countered the public's attraction to the theory. Indeed, even though many political theorists cringe at the thought of basing the design and analysis of social institutions upon what Joseph Schumpeter described as "the shallowest of all conceivable philosophies of life" (quoted in Mack, 1963, 2), the work of politicians and policy analysts routinely reflects this perspective, and the public rarely complains. This is not to deny the plausibility of philosophical critiques that argue that the emphasis on individual happiness may diminish the attention paid to family, personal integrity, true friendships, hard work, and other virtuous goals. But the public often finds it difficult to explain the fundamental value of such goals without ultimately referencing happiness.

Critics do question the notion of measuring a goal as elusive as happiness. They point to the inadequacy of using proxies such as GNP to measure aggregate happiness and to policy analysts' inability to measure or predict the impact of different policies on aggregate happiness. These difficulties, however, lead to calls for more appropriate proxies and more accurate measures, not for abandoning this kind of analysis. In the end, the notion that social policies should be judged by their impact on aggregate well-being hardly seems like a choice. As Hanna Pitkin (1990) notes, "Some of Bentham's ideas have become commonplace assumptions, to the point where one might say that Bentham has triumphed within each of us" (105).

Since it is often difficult to fully understand that which seems self-evident, it makes sense to take a step back and consider this theory's grounding and its implications for policy. Bentham's goal was to develop a scientific approach that permitted reasoned thought to direct government actions and, more generally, to inform moral decisions.

His utilitarian theory declared that happiness was the ultimate good. Happiness was defined as the excess of pleasure over pain. Pleasures might differ in quantity and intensity but not in quality. He wanted to structure society so as to promote the greatest good for the greatest number (Bentham, [1776] 1969). Economists' attention to utility is driven by a similar logic. Optimal outcomes are those which, for a given set of resources, maximize utility.

The theory grew out of the Enlightenment era and, as a result, reflected commitments to empiricism, individualism, rationalism, and neutrality with respect to the good. Thus Bentham and other utilitarians argued that both individuals and governments should base their behavior on empirical estimations of the pleasure and pain associated with varied actions. Their commitment to neutrality meant that neither governments nor other institutions (such as organized religion) should dictate the legitimacy of differing sources of pleasure or pain. Also central to utilitarian ethical systems is a commitment to rationality. Rational individuals are assumed to be utility maximizers.

Despite this common ground, utilitarians disagree about some important issues. John Stuart Mill ([1863] 1957) argued, for example, that analysts should recognize qualitative differences among pleasures. He believed that some pleasures, such as those associated with intellectual pursuits, were of a higher order than others:

> It is better to be a human being dissatisfied than a fool satisfied. And if the fool, or the pig, are of a different opinion, it is because they know only their side of the question. (Mill, [1863] 1957, 9)

This approach permits Mill to respond to the common criticism of utilitarians that they understand virtue to be nothing more than the pursuit of pleasure—a hedonistic calculus. Mill's tact is a departure from Bentham's contention that a mindless activity such as pushpin might be as valuable as reading poetry.

The twentieth-century English philosopher G. E. Moore and other "ideal" utilitarians take this critique even further than Mill does. Ideal utilitarians reject hedonistic utilitarians' conclusion that pleasure should be the sole criterion of utility. Rather than making distinctions between higher-order and lower-order pleasures as Mill does, these theorists put forward a set of intellectual and aesthetic priorities. They argue that certain pleasant states that conflicted with intellectual and aesthetic goals might lessen aggregate utility.

There are other debates as well. Some utilitarians endorse "act" utilitarianism, while others argue for "rule" utilitarianism. Act utilitarians judge the desirability of each individual action by weighing its consequences. Rule utilitarians assess the consequences associated with particular categories of actions, such as obeying laws or being truthful. Utilitarians also differ in the emphasis they place on creating policies that promote total utility versus those that seek to promote average utility. Analysts who focus on total utility often formulate inclusive policies. By increasing the number of individuals who receive a given service, whether access to a particular swimming pool or a particular teacher, they can increase the total utility. Others worry that as the size of the group served by a particular teacher or a swimming pool expands, the quality of services participating individuals receive falls and this lowers average utility. Utilitarians also support a wide range of different proxies for utility. When assessing the utility associated with an educational experience, for example, they might focus on proxies that include measures of academic achievement, increased earning potential, student satisfaction, student happiness, or the amount paid for such services (see Smart and Williams, 1973, and Sen and Williams, 1982, for a more detailed exploration of these and related issues).

Despite these differences, utilitarians are united in their commitment to promoting the greatest good for the greatest number, their association of utility with individuals (a group's utility is the aggregate of the utility experienced by individuals), and their adoption of an ethical system in which government should ask individuals to sacrifice some utility if such actions will raise the aggregate utility of community members.

Conceptually, this orientation combines two different kinds of theories: welfarism and consequentialism (see Sen and Williams, 1982, 3). Welfarism derives from the welfare of the individual: It assigns values to different states of affairs based on an assessment of individuals' satisfaction, preferences, or utility. Consequentialists judge the desirability of an action by evaluating its impact on the welfare of an individual or a group. They do not judge an action by considering its inherent value as, say, a virtue, a sin, or an end in itself. Suppose, for example, that policy makers wished to assess the desirability of hiring more police officers. Their commitment to welfarism would lead them to estimate the impact of this policy on the well-being of various groups of citizens. Their calculations would involve the costs and benefits associated with such factors as increased safety, employment opportunities, and tax burden. This analysis would be complicated since the impact on individual welfare depends on whether a citizen already feels safe, resents taxation, or commits crimes. Moreover, individual welfare is often affected by perceptions as well as realities. Additional police may raise aggregate welfare by improving citizens' sense of security even if their actual level of safety remains relatively constant. Utilitarians' consequentialist beliefs would lead them to focus more on the outcome of a given policy than on the policy as an end in its own right. Thus, they would assess whether additional police officers would increase or decrease aggregate welfare. They would be less directly concerned with whether hiring police was a fair or caring way to respond to crime and the social conditions that promote it.

Utilitarian principles work well as a frame for policy deliberations. Our culture values progress, pleasure, and productivity. Economists, policy analysts, and the public frequently equate utility with productivity and measure it in dollars. As a result, utility is widely recognized as a legitimate and important focus for policy makers. Furthermore, the quest for legitimacy leads administrators and policy analysts to give more attention to goals that can be specified, monitored, easily discussed, and maximized than to goals with features less amenable to "scientific" analysis (see Majone, 1989). The analytic logic used by utilitarians aligns well with this preference for decision-making procedures that appear rational, oriented toward progress, and scientific. Indeed, as Pitkin (1990) points out, public choice theory, rational choice theory, game theory, and cost–benefit analysis are all consistent with utilitarian philosophy—as are neoclassical economics and much modern political science. Bentham's model has certainly proved influential.

This is not to say that all players in a policy process measure utility according to the same criteria. However, those who adopt an analytic framework in line with utilitarian beliefs can discuss complex and contentious policy issues in ways consistent with our culture's commitment to rationality and science. These analysts may disagree on both the appropriateness of various proxies for utility and the desirability of various policies, but they are likely to be comfortable with the analytic method (e.g., measurement of specifiable outcomes, cost–benefit analysis, and maximization) used by utilitarians.

UTILITARIAN THOUGHT AND EDUCATIONAL POLICY

Although educational analysis consistent with a utilitarian paradigm need not emphasize the economic value of schooling, most does. Utilitarians emphasize the ability of schools to increase our material well-being. They view education as both a public and a private good, and they equate individual and group productivity with utility. Analysts assume that productivity increases our material resources and security. This material wealth makes us happy, satisfies our basic needs, and facilitates our pursuit of happiness.

"Human capital theory" embodies utilitarian commitments and places the value of education within a neoclassical economic framework. This framework lets economists model the way different factors can alter an individual's commitment to various educational endeavors and the impact of such decision processes on economic development. For example, if education promotes cognitive development and if cognitive development promotes productivity, then individuals can be expected to assess the desirability of marginal additions in educational attainment or achievement by weighing the costs (time, money, effort, and headaches, for example) and the benefits (job opportunities, income, and status) and, in the process, to maximize their utility. Similarly, a national education policy might be assessed by examining its costs (such as subsidizing education) versus its benefits (increasing productivity or international economic competitiveness).

Cognitive development, skill development, socialization, and attainment of credentials all receive the attention of educators and analysts who focus on human capital. Although the term "human capital" gained prominence in the 1960s (Becker, 1964), this general orientation was not new. Jones and Williamson (1979) argue that in the late nineteenth century a shift occurred regarding the aim of mass education in England. Discourse concerning goals shifted from promoting "habits of integrity and prudence" (Bernard, in Jones and Williamson, 69) to training children in skills (Jones and Williamson, 102). In the early twentieth century, educators in the United States such as David Snedden and Ellwood P. Cubberley emphasized these goals when they argued that "the school must . . . come to realize that its real worth and adequate reward lies in its social efficiency" (Cubberley, 1909, 54).

Although modern versions of this utilitarian rhetoric differ somewhat from their historical counterparts, concern for human capital development remains an explicit part of modern policy rhetoric. In the 1983 report *A Nation at Risk*, we were told, for example:

> The risk is not only that the Japanese make automobiles more efficiently than Americans . . . that the South Koreans recently built the world's most efficient steel mill. . . . It is also that these developments signify a redistribution of trained capability throughout the globe. (National Commission for Excellence in Education, 6–7)

Similarly, David Kearns, the former chairman of Xerox who became the deputy secretary of education, summarized the thinking of many in the business community when he said:

> The public schools are suppliers of our workforce.... But they're suppliers with a 50 percent defect rate. A fourth of our kids drop out; another fourth graduate barely able to read their own diplomas. (Kearns, 1988)

When researchers and practitioners try to maximize learning outcomes or when they try to minimize[1] dropouts, when they speak of changes in aggregate test scores or in attendance rates, when they talk about aligning the school's curriculum with the demands of the modern economy, and when they focus on the aggregate costs and benefits of a particular intervention, they are speaking in ways that are consistent with a utilitarian framework. Utilitarian themes of efficiency and productivity remain central frames for modern policy discussions.

Utilitarian analysis need not focus on these issues. Indeed, it is ironic that a theory that emphasizes happiness is most commonly used in educational policy discussions in ways that downplay a focus on pleasure. For example, policy analysts rarely write about students' joy in relation to a particular school activity unless a connection is made between that joy and academic accomplishments. In fact, rhetoric about joy as an end in its own right would probably undermine the legitimacy of a policy document.

Bentham, for his part, was clear that schools could pursue utility in two distinct ways. Schools could help individuals increase their capacity to pursue happiness through cognitive and skill development, or they could promote the kinds of attitudes toward others that would make for a happier society: "[Benevolence] is in great measure the produce of cultivation, the fruit of education" (Bentham, [1843] 1962, 561). This means of promoting happiness rarely receives systematic attention from policy analysts. Similarly, although educators occasionally speak of the importance of exposing all children to Shakespeare, Mill's commitment to "higher pleasures" and the attainment of ideal utilitarians' priorities are not carefully monitored by policy analysts. Analysts may give lip service to the importance of knowledge, benevolence, and the arts, but their analysis generally focuses on "the bottom line"— aggregate measures of school achievement and completion.

A CONCERN FOR RIGHTS AND JUSTICE

While concern for promoting utility occupies a privileged space within the realm of social policy discussions, it has one prominent rival— justice. To say that a policy or a feature of our social institutions is unjust is to say that it is wrong and should change. As John Rawls (1971) puts it, "Justice is the first principle of social institutions, as truth is of systems of thought" (3). Of course, the nature of justice and its implications for policy and policy analysis are profoundly controversial. As a culture, we may agree that justice is good and injustice is bad, but that consensus fades as soon as specific dilemmas are discussed.

Neutrality with Respect to "the Good"

Rights theorists focus on justice and individual rights, while utilitarians put utility first. Both groups of theorists, however, share the liberal commitment to an educational program that does not dictate a particular vision of the good life. That is, both groups grant individuals the authority to define and pursue their own priorities. This perspective has significant implications for educators. For example, an educational program that restricts children's access to alternative perspectives and experiences is largely inconsistent with the principles of most rights theorists. How is a child to freely develop his or her own opinions, interests, and abilities, without access to a diverse range of perspectives and opportunities? For this reason, rights theorists generally hope to provide students access to a wide range of curricular choices and to varied perspectives on any given issue (see Gutmann, 1982, and Strike, 1991). As a result, although rights theorists are not consequentialists generally, when evaluating educational policies they do attend to consequences. They worry about whether a particular educational experience "expands or contracts the opportunities children will have for rational choice in the future" (Gutmann, 1982, 268).

Thus, rights theorists can remain committed to individual liberty without granting children absolute control over their own education. Policy makers, teachers, or parents who are committed to individual liberty can still limit and focus a student's attention. Such restrictions frequently will be unavoidable (schools can offer only so many curricular options), desirable (parents and professionals often will be better judges of what experiences will enable students to make free and informed decisions as adults), and just (children are not adults and thus need not always be accorded the same degree of freedom).

The policy directions implied by commitments to individual liberty and justice are also heavily dependent on the relationship posited between education and life. To the extent that education (particularly schooling) is viewed as life, then educators must value the time students spend in school as an end in its own right. In such circumstances it becomes hard to justify constraints on students' autonomy on the grounds that certain required experiences will prepare the students for their life after school. On the other hand, if education is viewed as preparation for life or if students are judged to be too young to be accorded full liberty, then students can be told what to do. The goal, in these instances, is to prepare students to guide their adult life in a rational and informed manner. Finally, when education is viewed as a means of compensating children for inequities in life that occur outside of school, then procedurally unequal treatment (special programs for poor children, for example) can be justified.

Educators can adopt more than one of these positions at a time. They can try to prepare students for life as free and rational individuals and at the same time try to compensate students for the unequal treatment they receive in other parts of society, but some conflicts will arise. In part, policy talk on the desirability of affirmative action reflects this kind of tension. Some, who view education as part of life, believe justice requires that future educational opportunities be based solely on prior educational performance. They believe programs that have different admission standards for different categories of students are unfair. Others believe a just system would structure educational opportunities so as to compensate for both educational and noneducational inequalities that exist in the society. They are more supportive of affirmative action policies.

Equality and Equality of Opportunity

Affirmative action is but one example of educational policy analysts' need to confront a central question: How can schools promote equality?

The promotion of both equality and equality of opportunity has long been seen as the primary means through which schools can foster a more just society. Horace Mann's vision of schools as the "great equalizer" has been put forward repeatedly during the past century and a half to justify expansion of and improvements in the provision of public schooling. However, although equality of outcome and particularly equality of opportunity have been fundamental concerns for educational policy makers (see Tyack and Hansot, 1982; Kirst, 1984), "the meaning of equality in education appears various and fugitive" (Kirp, 1982, 32). Moreover, the policy implications of these differing definitions are substantial (Coleman, 1968; Gutmann, 1987).

Delineations between understandings of equality and equality of opportunity can be drawn in a variety of ways. Rawls's (1971) framework, in particular, facilitates and clarifies distinctions that are of particular relevance for educational policy makers. The scheme involves a grid showing four visions of the just society—natural liberty, natural aristocracy, liberal equality, and democratic equality[2]—characterized by two (not unrelated) tensions:

- *Equality as equality of careers open to talents versus equality as equality of fair opportunity.* Proponents of equality of careers open to talents maintain that access to positions or careers should depend on ability, and not on race, class, sex, friendships, nepotism, and so forth. Those who define equality as equality of fair opportunity argue that positions should be open in the formal sense (i.e., careers open to talents) and, in addition, "those with similar abilities and skills should have similar life chances" (Rawls, 1971, 73). Life circumstances, being born to a poor family, for example, should not influence the likelihood that one can develop the talents necessary to compete.
- *Principle of efficiency versus difference principle.* Under the principle of efficiency, arrangements are judged efficient so long as no individual's position can be improved without simultaneously lowering the desirability of a different individual's position (see Rawls, 1971, 67–72). Under the difference principle, "social and economic inequalities are to be arranged so that they are both (1) to the greatest benefit of the least advantaged, consistent with the just savings principle (efficiency), and (2) attached to offices and positions open to all under conditions of fair equality of opportunity" (Rawls, 1971, 302).

System of Natural Liberty or Libertarianism. The system of natural liberty reflects commitments to efficiency and to equality as careers open to talents. Libertarian analysts see individual freedom as their ultimate goal and, rather than focusing on the impact that the social, economic, and cultural milieu can have on opportunities, they value individual rights. Libertarians argue that no state or other body can justly mandate transfers between individuals. Thus, they criticize legislative efforts to redistribute wealth or opportunities even if such actions might promote greater happiness, equality, or equality of opportunity. Laws that redistribute wealth violate the efficiency principle by sacrificing one individual's utility in an attempt to promote the well-being of others. In essence, libertarians put the rights of the givers above those of recipients. Nozick (1974) summarizes this position:

> The major objection to speaking of everyone's having a right to various things such as equality of opportunity, life and so on, and enforcing this right, is that these "rights" require a substructure of things and materials and actions; and other people may have rights and entitlement over these. No one has a right to something whose realization requires certain uses of things and activities that other people have rights and entitlement over. (238)

Consequently, only voluntary transfers are viewed as just. Libertarians work to limit government regulation and to promote a free market system. Although they would support legislation that mandates that "careers be open to talents," by, for example, outlawing racial, gender, or class discrimination in the workplace, they would not be comfortable with more intrusive means of promoting equality. What might this mean for education?

Much educational policy discourse endorses libertarian conceptions of individual rights. Libertarians support the widely accepted belief that students should compete for varied credentials, grades, and future educational opportunities. In addition, although libertarians value freedom, a coercive schooling environment, one in which student choice is significantly constrained, could be consistent with libertarian thought. Libertarians can argue that children are too young to be afforded absolute freedom. They might support a coercive school environment as long as parents and not public agencies selected it. For parents to justify this coercion they would have to argue that their policy choice would, in the long run, promote students' liberty.

With respect to matters of school governance, libertarians want free markets, not government regulation. Their preference for market control over public policy initiatives would likely lead them to support reformers who propose relatively unregulated voucher systems (see Hayek, 1976, 84), ones in which students or their parents choose their own schools. They might ask the state to ensure that students have fair access to educational opportunities, but, once access was guaranteed, they would try to prevent the state from using policy to regulate or shape the kinds of opportunities students or parents selected. In important respects, the phrase "libertarian policy making" is a contradiction in terms.

Liberal Equality or Meritocracy. Many moral philosophers criticize the libertarian emphasis on individuals' property rights. They point out that while free markets may make individuals with resources "free to choose" (Friedman and Friedman, 1979), free markets may also leave those without resources "free to lose" to others who have an unfair advantage (Roemer, 1988). Responses to this dilemma vary—some aim to promote liberal equality. That is, rather than working to limit government intervention, they see government as a means of promoting a relatively level playing field in which "free" markets can function fairly. These systems of liberal equality or meritocracy aim to provide individuals a "fair opportunity" to compete for desired goals and, at the same time, adhere to the principle of efficiency. Meritocrats are comfortable with unequal results so long as all are given an equal opportunity to succeed or fail.

For generations schools have been promoted as one of the government's chief mechanisms for fostering meritocracy. Thomas Jefferson,[3] for example, proposed an organizational structure for public schools in Virginia that would grant all students (boys and girls) access to three years of schooling and then select the most academically talented male student from each school for additional education. Ultimately, by selecting the best student from each level of schooling, the process would identify the top 20 male students and provide them a full and free public education. "By this means," Jefferson wrote, "twenty of the best geniuses will be raked annually from the rubbish" (in Tozer, Violas, and Senese, 1993, 30).

Rather than emphasizing the sorting features of a meritocracy, many policy analysts and advocates argue that in order to enable meritocratic competition after schooling, educators must provide all students with comparable educational opportunities. Proposals to promote more equitable financing both between and within school districts are put forward with this view of equity in mind. For example,

> The Supreme Court found that wide variation in financial resources had created unequal educational opportunities throughout Kentucky and that these disparate opportunities crippled the educational attainment of students who lived in property-poor districts. (Benson, 1991, 417)

Head Start programs and other strategies that attempt to compensate or offset the influence of economic, social, and cultural factors affecting children's performance in school are also attempts to promote meritocracy. Coleman espoused a similar goal in his influential study aptly titled "Equality of Educational Opportunity" and also known as the "Coleman Report":

The effectiveness of the schools consists, in part, of making the conditional probabilities less conditional—that is, less dependent upon social origins. Thus, equality of educational opportunity implies, not merely "equal" schools, but equally effective schools, whose influences will overcome the differences in starting point of children from different social groups. (Coleman, 1966, 72)

A Rawlsian View of Kantian Justice or Democratic Equality. Rawls (1971) offers an alternative to utilitarianism, libertarianism, and meritocracy in his seminal work *A Theory of Justice.* He faults utilitarians for violating individual rights when they attempt to maximize aggregate utility, libertarians for permitting distribution of positions and rewards to be influenced "by ... factors [both native abilities and social and economic status] so arbitrary from a moral point of view" (72), and those who support meritocratic systems because he feels the distribution of natural assets is every bit as arbitrary as that of social assets. "Equality of opportunity," he writes, "means an equal chance to leave the less fortunate behind in the personal quest for influence and social position" (106–7).

One must consider how Rawls arrives at his alternative to libertarian and meritocratic visions of justice in order to understand his conclusion. He engages in a thought experiment. He asks readers to imagine the principles for organizing society they would create if they did not know their social class, social status, physical abilities, or intelligence, but did know all relevant facts about society and had a strong understanding of the social and behavioral sciences. This, he argues, provides a fair setting in which to consider various alternatives. He concludes that a rational individual under this "veil of ignorance" in what he calls the "original position" would select two principles:

First Principle
Each person is to have an equal right to the most extensive system of equal basic liberties compatible with a similar system of liberty for all.

Second Principle
Social and economic inequalities are to be arranged so that they are both:
    (a) to the greatest benefit of the least advantaged, consistent with the just savings principle, and
    (b) attached to offices and positions open to all under conditions of fair equality of opportunity. (Rawls, 1971, 302)

General Conception
All social primary goods—liberty and opportunity, income and

wealth, and the bases of self-respect—are to be distributed equally
unless an unequal distribution of any or all of these goods is to the
advantage of the least favored. (303)

The priority ordering of the principles is principle 1, then 2b, and
then 2a. This means that those designing policies should work first to
ensure the basic liberties (freedom of conscience, of thought, of speech
and assembly, the right to vote—see p. 61) described in principle 1.
Next, they should focus on promoting fair equality of opportunity
(principle 2b). This goal requires that those with similar skills have
access to similar careers. Moreover, life circumstances (such as being
born into a poor family) should not diminish an individual's opportunity to develop talents. Then, once those concerns are met, policy
would be guided by the desire to maximize the welfare of the least
advantaged (principle 2a). This priority, also known as "the difference
principle," requires that policy makers focus not on promoting average
or total utility, but on promoting the well-being of the least well off.

In terms of education, this commitment to the worst off would not
necessarily mean that relatively more successful or "gifted" students
would be neglected. Indeed, they might get extra services:

> [T]he difference principle would allocate resources in education, say,
> so as to improve the long-term expectations of the least favored. If
> this end is attained by giving more attention to the better endowed,
> it is permissible; otherwise not. (Rawls, 1971, 101)

In other words, if a subsidized honors program benefited less well-off
citizens (through gains in national productivity or medical advances)
more than a subsidized dropout prevention program, the honors program would be funded.

If one were to follow this model, the emphasis educators place
on meritocracy also would be abandoned. However, incentives tied to
performance would remain and would be structured to promote behavior that improved the welfare of the worst off. Consequently, talented or hard working citizens could be rewarded if these incentives
improved (presumably through increased output) the lives of the least
well off.

In addition, although Rawls avoids, and indeed attacks, meritocratic notions of justice, he comes to some conclusions that are similar
to Coleman's. Specifically, like Coleman he wishes to compensate those
"born into less favorable social positions" (poor people, members of
oppressed minority groups, and so on). Unlike Coleman he also
wishes to compensate "those with fewer native assets." In his words:

> [I]n order to treat all persons equally, to provide genuine equality of opportunity, society must give more attention to those with fewer native assets and to those born into the less favorable social positions. The idea is to redress the bias of contingencies in the direction of equality. In pursuit of this principle greater resources might be spent on the education of the less rather than the more intelligent. (Rawls, 1971, 100–1)

Given the significance of socialization in the educational process, the limits Rawls places on educators interested in changing student beliefs are of particular relevance:

> Imagine two persons in full possession of their reason and will who affirm different religious or philosophical beliefs; and suppose that there is some psychological process that will convert each to the other's view, despite the fact that the process is imposed on them against their wishes . . . let us suppose, both come to accept conscientiously their new beliefs. We are still not permitted to submit them to this treatment. (Rawls, 1971, 249–50)

Rawls believes that "moral education is education for autonomy" (516) and, although it may be fostered through "paternalistic intervention," it can be justified only if it "reflects the subject's more permanent aims and preferences" (250). The understandings or attitudes promoted must be ones that the individuals would accept independently on reasonable grounds (516). In other words, parents can guide their child's educational plan when the child is not able to rationally consider the impact of various choices on his or her long-range priorities. Those with this view might criticize the practices of many religious schools for their commitment to socializing students to accept particular religious doctrine. They also would assess cautiously public policy rhetoric emphasizing the importance of teaching students to accept culturally specific understandings of what are often called "basic moral values."

EQUITY AS A MEANS TO PROMOTE UTILITY, RATHER THAN AS AN END IN ITSELF

Although the three conceptions of equality discussed above are all supported by appeals to fairness and rights, it is important to note that educational philosophers who promote equality often appeal to utility rather than to rights. R. M. Hare (1982) offers a utilitarian justification of attention to rights. He points to two factors that frequently will lead utilitarians to promote equity. First, most economists accept the notion that individuals experience diminishing marginal utility for both commodities and money. As a result, a more equitable distribution of money and commodities frequently will increase total utility. In addition, he writes that "inequalities tend to produce . . . envy, hatred and malice, whose disutility needs no emphasizing" (Hare, 1982, 27). A second kind of argument in favor of equality mentioned by Hare (1977) is more commonly made by economists who point out that education is a public good as well as a private good. Such analysts argue that the unequal outcomes of our educational system frequently lead many to drop out and to be poorly educated. This result has high social costs (lower economic productivity, crime, and so on), which lower aggregate utility.

Henry Levin (1990) has placed concern for equality squarely within a utilitarian framework. He puts forward a social utility function in which total utility is the sum of national income and the degree of societal equality. In this model utility is the goal, and equality becomes a means to that end.

Inclusion of these utilitarian justifications is important because not all references to the importance of equality use the logic or goals of rights theorists. In fact, these utilitarian orientations closely approximate much of the rhetoric used in educational policy discussions to promote both equality and equality of opportunity.

Educational policy analysts attend to equity, efficiency, and excellence. These priorities reflect the dominance of utilitarian thought and rights-based concerns for justice. The consensus on use of this rhetoric, however, is misleading. As noted above, multiple and significantly different priorities can be attached to pleas for equity, efficiency, and excellence. Each word can have a variety of meanings. The differences associated with varied understandings of equity are particularly consequential.

Unfortunately, these distinctions are frequently ignored by analysts and policy makers. Analysts who use the language of utility and rights generally adopt narrow understandings of educational growth that emphasize the importance of human capital development. The lack of attention accorded other interpretations of utility and justice constrains the public's ability to assess the desirability of different policy directions. Further, when analysts accept equity, excellence, and efficiency as the frame for policy discussions, they often neglect other individual and social priorities. In Chapters 3 and 4, I consider two of these alternatives.

3
Communitarian Thought

The loyalties which once held individuals, which gave them support,
direction and unity of outlook on life, have well-nigh disappeared. In
consequence, individuals are confused and bewildered. It would be difficult to find in history an epoch as lacking in solid and assured objects
of belief and approved ends of action as is the present.

—John Dewey, *Individualism Old and New*

Today we see the weakening and collapse of communities of obligations
and commitment, and of coherent belief systems. We see a loss of a
sense of identity and belonging, of opportunities for allegiance, for being
needed and responding to need—and a corresponding rise in feelings
of alienation, impotence, and anomie.

—John Gardner, *Building Community*

Utilitarian and rights theories reflect the Enlightenment's emphasis on
rational autonomous individuals. Utilitarians measure the utility or
happiness of individual citizens and strive to maximize the aggregate
utility of a given population. Rights theorists attempt to ensure that
individuals can freely pursue their own goals so long as this pursuit
does not constrain another individual's freedom. In contrast, communitarians criticize this focus on autonomous individuals. They feel notions of autonomy understate the degree to which an individual's goals
and qualities are formed by the community. They stress the benefits of
harmonious, cohesive, and supportive communities in which individuals share goals and obligations.

A BRIEF OUTLINE OF COMMUNITARIAN THOUGHT

Plato's philosophical, political, and educational theories embody traditional communitarian commitments.[1] Rather than placing priority on
the creation of social institutions that respond to individual desires or
protect individual rights, Plato's "good society" was designed to foster
harmonious interactions among citizens and to further common goals.

He recognized individual differences, but understood their significance in terms of the different social roles they implied. He believed that social harmony became possible when individuals acted in accordance with specified, complementary, and hierarchically arranged roles. Plato's system was one in which some were laborers and traders, others defended the state, and a third group, those with the greatest intellectual capacity, guided the government. He hoped that individuals would receive educational experiences that prepared them for the roles they were to assume.

During the Enlightenment, a new ideology endorsing notions of individual autonomy achieved prominence. Social critics during this period argued that many of the fixed roles and hierarchical structures of traditional social institutions violated individuals' natural rights and constrained their pursuit of happiness. They placed less emphasis on the community and more on matters of utility and individual rights. Such concerns structure modern justifications for public policy initiatives (see MacIntyre, 1981).

Although most economists, political theorists, and moral philosophers since the Enlightenment have championed the benefits of this new individualistic orientation, substantial concerns also have been raised. Critics charge that this emphasis on the autonomy of individuals has helped to foster the sense of rootlessness, isolation, and alienation so many citizens experience (see, for example, Tocqueville [1848] 1966; Dewey, 1930; Bellah et al., 1985). Others have worried that liberal notions of individual rights promote oppressive forms of inequality. As Rousseau explains in *Discourse on the Origin of Inequality* ([1755] 1967), the prevailing conceptualization of individual rights and liberties, particularly the right to private property, dissolves the social bond and fosters a competitive situation in which "a handful gorge themselves with superfluities, while the starving masses lack the barest necessities of life" (246).

Dewey's view, although moderate in comparison with Rousseau's, exemplifies the substantial nature of communitarian concerns:

> Individuals who are not bound together in associations, whether domestic, economic, religious, political, artistic, or educational, are monstrosities. It is absurd to suppose that the ties which hold them together are merely external and do not react to mentality and character, producing the framework of personal disposition. The tragedy of the "lost individual" is due to the fact that while individuals are now caught up into a vast complex of associations, there is no harmonious and coherent reflection of the import of these connections into the imaginative and emotional outlook on life. (Dewey, 1930, 80–81)

In short, communitarians reject the notion that citizens exist as autonomous entities within society.[2] They believe that individual preferences both shape and are shaped by the communities in which people live. These theorists worry that an orientation that emphasizes autonomy and individual rights prevents progress toward the "good society" by fostering competition, envy, alienation, and selfishness among citizens. It also creates "lost individuals" who lack common goals and the meaning, support, and direction that flow from membership in a community.

TWO SCHOOLS OF THOUGHT

Communitarians hope to foster social environments in which the actions and motivations of individuals are in harmony with societal needs. Rather than creating settings in which individuals work at cross-purposes as they pursue narrow understandings of self-interest, they want individuals to work together toward common goals. They endorse Aristotle's belief that people realize their full humanity through association with one another.

Communitarian political theorists have not, however, reached consensus on the degree to which traditional roles, responsibilities, and community norms should guide/constrain the behavior of individuals. One group, which I will call "traditional communitarians," adopt much of Plato's and Aristotle's emphasis on traditional roles and responsibilities. The second group follows John Dewey[3] and promotes a vision of community in which a rational and democratic decision-making process enables the pursuit of shared goals. These "democratic communitarians" want community norms and values continually held open to informed critique. They expect change as knowledge and public sentiments shift.

I will argue that philosophers during the Enlightenment were right to reject traditional communitarian logics and goals. Although the traditional communitarian critique of liberalism remains powerful and demonstrates the need for an alternative to liberalism, traditional communitarian thought fails to provide a desirable structure for policy analysts. Dewey's democratic communitarian vision offers a more viable alternative. In what follows, I describe these two schools of communitarian thought and consider their implications for educational policy makers.

MODERN PROPONENTS OF "TRADITIONAL" COMMUNITIES

Modern proponents of "traditional" communities hope that the maintenance and/or resurrection of traditional values, beliefs, roles, and responsibilities will foster social harmony and provide individuals with a more meaningful and morally tenable life. Alasdair MacIntyre (1981), for example, states that the relativist logic of utilitarian and rights theorists leaves us without the language or set of principles needed to guide our lives in a morally coherent manner. He believes that a return to a society with a shared conception of the good is necessary in order to develop a coherent set of moral principles. Only when citizens join or develop associations in which members accept relatively similar ethical goals and understandings, can ethical evaluation resolve disputes.

Allan Bloom (1987) makes a related argument in his unanticipated best-seller *The Closing of the American Mind*. He argues that our institutions of higher learning no longer engage students in a common search for the nature of "the good." Instead they promote a vision of "openness" that "is open to all kinds of men, all kinds of life-styles, all ideologies" (27). Bloom faults this pluralist and relativist liberal orientation, which he feels drives both curriculum and pedagogy at elite institutions. Modern-day liberals deprive students of access to what Bloom regards as our "shared" heritage. They teach individuals that "their beliefs do not entitle them as individuals, or collectively as a nation, to think they are superior to anyone else" (30). This perspective, he argues, leads educators to prevent students from seeking the nature of the good because it also would lead to "discovery of the bad and contempt for it" (30). As a result, students develop a kind of tolerance but not a shared understanding of the public good.

Actors in the political arena also have championed the need to refer to one's traditions when confronting moral questions. Political appeals to "traditional family values," to "love of country," and to various religious beliefs are neither new nor confined to a particular political party. In recent times, Ronald Reagan, George Bush, and Dan Quayle have offered the most politically marketable argument for these perspectives. They describe the courts, the media, and government bureaucracies as powerful but detached public institutions that diminish the community's ability to maintain commitments to family, church, and tradition. They also fault liberal politicians for adopting permissive and relativistic attitudes that are inconsistent with "traditional family values" and that fail to provide citizens with moral guidance.

Educational Implications of a "Traditional" Communitarian Perspective

In one of his earliest writings, "Discourse on Political Economy," published in Diderot's *Encyclopedia*, Rousseau describes an extreme communitarian vision in which individual identities dissolve and students adopt the community's goals as their own:

> If they [children] are trained early enough never to consider their own persons except in terms of their relations with the body of the state, and not to perceive of their own existence, so to speak, except as a part of the state, they may finally succeed in identifying themselves in some way with this greater whole . . . and thus transforming into a sublime virtue that dangerous disposition from which all our vices arise. (in Ritter and Bondanella, 1988, 73)

Proposals along these lines would have few supporters today. Neither educators nor the general public encourage this kind of transformative educational experience. However, some do support an educational agenda that aligns with traditional communitarian commitments. These advocates worry that modern individuals have lost their ties to the past, to traditional values, and to one another. They believe that the schools provide an important means with which to respond. Educational institutions can provide access to both the style and the substance of a particular tradition. They can teach the skills needed to further both community and individual goals. Finally, school practices can help establish and demonstrate the value of strong ties to one's community and to its members.

An Example: Amish Education

The structure and practices of Amish schools reflect a relatively complete commitment to traditional communitarian values. The typical Amish parochial school rejects the individualist orientation that guides educational practice in the rest of this country. Their schools deemphasize individual differences. All students receive instruction based on the same curriculum, and no attempt is made to identify or reward students based on academic performance. In addition, the content of the curriculum reflects the perceived needs of the community rather than the interests of particular students. The curriculum stresses rote learning of basic skills, skills appropriate for the Amish's largely agrarian life style, and exposure to Amish religious values.

Pedagogic practice within these schools reflects a communitarian emphasis on interdependence. Peer learning, cross-age tutoring, and cooperative activities are all common. Competitive structures and rewards for students with special talents are viewed by the Amish as anti-Christian. Finally, their communitarian ethic is manifest in the tremendous involvement of parents in the running of the schools. Parents select and pay the teacher or teachers. Frequently, community members both build and maintain school buildings, and, on days when a teacher is ill, a parent often assumes the role of substitute teacher (Kachel, 1989; also see Hostetler, 1963; Fishman, 1987).[4]

Some Costs of "Traditional Harmony"

The peaceful and supportive structure of Amish schools might strike many as idyllic. It is important to note, however, that citizens in this supportive and nurturing community adhere to long-established norms that many readers might view as constraining and oppressive. For example, although the relations between husbands and wives are often respectful, gender distinctions have great significance in Amish society. Men run the farm and women run the household. Men control the finances and generally have the final word on important family decisions. Women are taught in accordance with "the biblical pattern: 'Wives, submit yourselves unto your own husband, as unto the Lord'" (Hostetler, 1963, 153).

These problematic dynamics are not unique to Amish society. Traditional communitarian values often foster hierarchical and caste-like social arrangements. Liberal theorists make the costs of these values quite clear. Their rejection of traditional communitarian thought turns on the belief that social "harmony" achieved through imposition of a hierarchically arranged set of fixed roles (defined by such factors as gender, caste, class, and race) constrains freedom and hampers individual and social development. Susan Okin (1979) reminds us, for example, that Aristotle's good society was one in which the intellectual and political activities of a privileged and all male group, required the subjugation of slaves, craftsmen, and women. In short, while traditional communities can provide individuals support, direction, and meaning, they also can be constraining, coercive, and exploitative.

Traditional Communitarian Thought in the Modern World

The problems faced when relatively homogeneous and stable societies adhere to tradition are amplified in modern contexts. Religious, ethnic, and cultural diversity, individual mobility, and rapid technological and cultural change mean that few citizens can be confident that their neighbors endorse or are even aware of their traditions. Policy agendas that invoke "tradition" as a rationale often embody the priorities and ideologies of a community's most powerful groups. They do not necessarily reflect widely shared beliefs. To the extent that a static traditional set of values, beliefs, and norms guides policy, this orientation is likely to be more a function of political power than of consensus.

Guiding a modern society by a particular tradition is thus both difficult and dangerous. Even Alasdair MacIntyre (1991), one of liberalism's harshest critics, concedes that "attempts to remake modern societies in systematically communitiarian ways will always be either ineffective or disastrous" (91). An alternative, however, is often supported: "What is possible and important," MacIntyre continues, "is for groups informed by an adequately shared conception of the human good to build community at the level of particular institutions—schools, farms, other workplaces, clinics, parishes" (91).

Following this logic, many hope to create publicly funded schools or programs with distinct cultural and/or religious orientations. Coons and Sugarman (1978) argue, for example, that the public should fund religious schools since nonsectarian settings must take neutral stands on values many parents view as central to a child's education. Similar sentiments also have been expressed by those who promote Afrocentric education (Hamilton, 1968; Lee, Lomotey, and Shujaa, 1990; Berger, 1991). In addition to helping maintain particular religious and cultural traditions, these schools aim to give students the support, direction, and esteem that stem from group membership.

Efforts to promote coherent communities in schools also can lead to a number of problems. Placing students, especially young students, in schools that endorse particular cultural norms and values may deny them access to alternative perspectives and constrain their ability to consider different visions of "the good." In addition, school cultures that grant primacy to one set of values constrain, if not oppress, those who hold alternative views. Such settings may have effects that extend beyond the school as well. They may lead mainstream students to develop and feel comfortable expressing contempt for those with other perspectives (see Strike, 1991, for discussion).

Both the appeal and the costs of structuring school practice around traditional communitarian commitments are quite real. Given the increasingly diverse nature of public life, such proposals should not be surprising. Historically, fear of diversity and change has led groups to try to insulate themselves from those with different values and beliefs. However, schools that insulate students from alternative perspectives threaten the creation and maintenance of democratic communities. Indeed, democratic communitarians might well argue that the same dynamics that currently make this emphasis on traditional communities popular, make its widespread acceptance dangerous.

PROPONENTS OF DEMOCRATIC COMMUNITIES

Not all who reject traditional communitarianism as a guide for public policy makers endorse liberal agendas. John Dewey, and those who build on his work, for example, reject the notion that political theorists must value either the individual or the community. This distinction, Dewey argues, is inappropriate and diminishes our ability to pursue both the good life and the good society. He wants educators to tailor their pedagogy and curriculum to the needs of individual children and, simultaneously, to forge miniature communities in which students work cooperatively toward common goals.

Dewey's Rejection of Both Traditional Communitarian Thought and Classical Liberalism

> No one could better express than [Plato] the fact that a society is stably organized when each individual is doing that for which he has aptitude by nature in such a way as to be useful to others (or to contribute to the whole to which he belongs); and that it is the business of education to discover these aptitudes and progressively to train them for social use. (Dewey, [1916] 1966, 88)

Although committed in many respects to Plato's vision, Dewey criticizes many features of the traditional communitarian perspective. First, such systems often require that individuals fit into static and narrowly defined roles. Dewey worries that these roles constrain individuals' efforts to reach their full potential. He also fears that traditional communitarian social arrangements are hierarchical and grant undue social status to the occupants of particular roles. Finally, Dewey is concerned that traditional communitarian social plans lack mechanisms through which a community can change and grow in response to either new knowledge or exposure to other cultures and perspectives.

However, while Dewey agrees with liberal critics who argue that traditional societies are often oppressive and constraining, he rejects the liberal alternative that emphasizes autonomy and individual rights. More specifically, Dewey argues that many liberal philosophers misinterpret the social movement associated with the Enlightenment period.

> Men were not actually engaged in the absurdity of striving to be free from connection with nature and one another. They were striving for greater freedom in nature and society. . . . They wanted to form their beliefs about it first hand, instead of through tradition. They wanted closer union with their fellows so that they might influence one another more effectively and might combine their respective actions for mutual aims. ([1916] 1966, 294)

As the opening line of this statement makes clear, Dewey rejects the notion of autonomous individuals. Communities shape individual values, perceptions, and options. They determine what individuals can "think of, plan, and choose" (1927, 75).

However, at the same time that Dewey appreciates the substantial formative influence of community norms on individual values and patterns of behavior, he also notes that individuals respond in different ways to similar stimuli. In fact, members of a community often adopt a broad range of values, beliefs, and interests. This diversity is desirable. It fosters reflection, debate, and experimentation, all of which drive progress. While recognizing this benefit, it is important to ensure that the conflict that understandably results from citizens' competing perspectives and priorities does not dissolve the social bond. Dewey hoped to promote what John Gardner (1990) calls "a wholeness incorporating diversity," in which individuals pursue different ends but maintain strong ties and commitments to one another.

As a result, practices that treat individuals as separate or somehow autonomous from the needs and influences of others within the society are inconsistent with his perspective. Dewey believes that individuals should work together toward common goals and that the needs of the community should help to structure students' educational programs. At the same time, Dewey criticizes traditional and static conceptions of community needs as well as attempts to maintain inflexible communal norms. He fears that these will constrain the growth of both individuals and communities.

In short, Dewey seeks a middle ground: a kind of balance that is theoretically appealing and elegant, but that is excruciatingly complex to pursue through practical steps. He believes that reformers and social theorists must recognize the way communities shape individuals, the importance of a shared vision, and the value of social harmony. But they also must respect diversity, abandon fixed roles, and recognize that the dissenting members of a community often foster its growth. As educators and others work to promote this balance, they help develop democratic communities.

Democratic Communities

There are, of course, numerous understandings of democracy. Most emphasize voting procedures and seek to create political structures that accord all citizens representation. Dewey, in contrast, views democracy as a way of life that extends far beyond formal participation in explicitly political institutions. His democratic project embodies a commitment to community. For him, democracy is a process, a mode of interaction among citizens: "The clear consciousness of a communal life, in all its implications, constitutes the idea of democracy" (1927, 149).

This statement, taken on its own, is misleading. Robbers, racists, and other groups might form strong communities and support one another. Only some kinds of communal arrangements get Dewey's support. In order to grasp Dewey's vision of democracy as a way of life, it is necessary to specify characteristics of the community he desires.

Dewey argues that two questions provide an internal and an external test for the desirability of a given community: "How numerous and varied are the interests which are consciously shared?" and "How full and free is the interplay with other forms of association?" ([1916] 1966, 83).

Since no specific set of institutional structures guarantees communities with these qualities, Dewey offers a rich description of these two goals and of the ways in which particular societal features and policy alternatives might be assessed. Instead of viewing these guidelines as formal principles, it makes sense to understand them as considerations that can inform policy deliberations in contextually varied settings.

Those who adopt Dewey's vision would seek policies that recognize and foster common interests among members. They would also support policies that facilitate critique of current norms through promotion of scientific investigations, open forums for discussion, and exposure to other groups. To many, this ideal might seem problematic. How can a community develop shared concerns if social and scientific critics constantly challenge consensus?

Dewey views community as a process, not a stagnant end. As community members struggle with both technical questions and explicitly normative dilemmas, they create community. What they share is a commitment to a process that aims to respond to society's needs through scientific inquiry, experimentation, and free discussion among all members. This process, which is the basis of community, does not require consensus regarding the importance or desirability of particular goals.

Consider the case of school-based decision making. To develop shared interests, participants must come to understand and value the needs and perspectives of other community members (administrators, teachers, parents, and students). To do this they will need to consider the effects of social, political, and economic structures on different groups' power and on their priorities. Lacking this orientation, social deliberations often turn into strategic efforts to further the interests of individuals and subgroups at the expense of the interests of others (teachers protect their autonomy, parents of "gifted" students push for their particular program, and so on). The development of shared interests is also threatened by status distinctions and differentials in cultural capital that limit participation in what should be public discussions. For instance, parents and students in poor neighborhoods often are only marginal players in school policy dialogues. They may be members of pro forma parent councils, but substantive discussions of school goals and ways to achieve them are handled by those who claim "professional" expertise (see McLaughlin and Shields, 1987). In contrast, when participants in the decision-making process inform their analysis with varied assessments of the nature of social needs and give space for all to participate, discussions, though at times contentious, can become a vital and enriching form of communal life. They provide forums in which participants develop shared understandings that can help them work toward a sense of common destiny and mutual aims.

This is not to say that such discussions will necessarily lead to consensus. In fact, it is doubtful that settings in which members all agree on all policy issues foster the reflection and diversity needed for growth. For this reason, exclusive and isolated communities which promote conformity rather than reflection and diversity are also rejected by democratic communitarians. Conformity, Dewey writes "[is] the artificial substitute used to hold men together" in the absence of dialogues that recognize differences in individual and group interests but which seek to accommodate them through shared decision-making (1930, 86). Thus, democratic communitarians criticize attempts to create schools or other institutions which promote traditional communitarian commitments. When agreement stems from a desire to conform to traditional patterns of behavior (whether a product of cultural norms, religious doctrine, or military protocol), the bonds which hold individuals together may constrain and distort individual growth. They will often prevent realization of many persons' talents and capacities by confining them to narrow patterns of thought and by asking them to fill prescribed roles.

Forging Democratic Communities in the Modern World

Today, diversity, technological change, mobility, and a cultural emphasis on autonomy all make creation of democratic communities even more difficult. As Strike (1989) states:

> People who live in a culture that has roots in Christianity, liberalism, and capitalism, and who within minutes can be assaulted by Jerry Falwell, deafened by MTV, manipulated by seductive appeals to purchase a wide variety of ego-inflating but useless products, and solicited to save the starving of Ethiopia, are unlikely to have inherited a very coherent, well-articulated set of moral concepts. (79)

Other contemporary analysts paint a similar picture. Bellah and his colleagues, in *Habits of the Heart* (1985), argue that our diminished sense of community is reflected in the way in which we talk about, understand, and guide our lives. More specifically, those authors worry that we may be losing the language and set of conceptual categories needed to understand our lives and goals in terms of our connections to loved ones and the broader public. They also highlight the degree to which the rationales individuals offer for both their behavior and their goals reflect an individual and often pecuniary sense of self-interest.

Social commentators charge that our inadequate communities are plainly evident in the prevalence of greed and destructive competition throughout society, in individuals' attempts to insulate themselves from community problems, and in the difficulties faced by those who try to create and sustain strong and supportive relationships both within the community and among family members (Gardner, 1990; Lasch, 1991; see also the Responsive Communitarian Platform, 1991/92, which was signed by dozens of noted academics and social activists). Their evidence includes stories of widespread public and private corruption, the flight of the middle class from cities to insular and often anonymous suburbs, and rising divorce rates.

Dewey was well aware of the challenges the modern era posed for those interested in fostering democratic communities. In *Individualism Old and New* (1930) he argued that the advent of the machine and mass production brought us into a collective age and gave new influence to industrial and business leaders. Consequently, "instead of the development of individualities . . . there is a perversion of the whole ideal of individualism to conform to the practices of a pecuniary culture" (18).

Dewey therefore argues for the creation of a new individualism, one more suitable for this modern age. Pursuit of this goal requires conscious institutionalization of procedures that downplay the emphasis of private gain and work to align individual goals, science, and technology with social ends. His vision also requires social practices and norms that embrace diversity as well as group obligation.

John Gardner (1990) revives this set of concerns. He offers a useful discussion and agenda for policy activists who, like himself, hope to promote modern communities that provide individuals with a sense of wholeness that incorporates diversity. There is a need, he writes, to create a "framework of shared purposes" that can simultaneously accommodate and include individuals with diverse backgrounds and preferences. This goal requires space for dissenters and for subcommunities with particular orientations. At the same time, the maintenance of a common agenda demands "institutional arrangements for diminishing polarization, for coalition-building, dispute resolution, negotiation and mediation" (16).

Gardner also notes that the rapid pace of technological change and the geographic mobility of individuals frequently alter traditions and communities. Thus, policy advocates interested in fostering communities within modern environments must consciously foster practices that generate new traditions and that forge meaningful and supportive relationships among a diverse population.

Gardner omits, however, a discussion relating these goals to economic structures. His model is less attentive than Dewey's to the ways economic arrangements and interests can promote both conflicts and destructive forms of individualism. Whether the issues concern neighborhood gentrification, construction of affordable housing, plant closings, affirmative action, or the development of health care policy, tensions between individuals' and groups' interests frequently make commitment to notions of the common interest difficult to maintain.

Amy Gutmann's (1987) liberal democratic vision of education, with its emphasis on nondiscrimination and nonrepression (44–45), aligns in important ways with Dewey's emphasis on free and full interplay with other forms of association. However, Gutmann's analysis centers on the question of who (the state, parents, professionals) should guide educational policy and on macro-policy issues such as busing, vouchers, and union influence. She does not provide an analysis of the pedagogical and curricular issues surrounding the design of democratic educational practices.

Implications for Educational Policy

Dewey felt that educational institutions were particularly well suited to help build and rebuild the sense of shared goals and obligations present in desirable communities. Indeed, schools could transform both individuals and societies. What kinds of concerns might those who share his communitarian perspective bring to the analysis of educational policy? One way into this arena is to examine how Dewey's pedagogic and curricular program reflects his communitarian and democratic commitments.

Communities as a Goal for Educators

Dewey wanted schools and teachers to provide more than access to the knowledge and culture of earlier generations. He hoped to foster transformative educational experiences that would develop among students a sense of mutual dependence and shared interests. These commitments led Dewey to place priority on educational goals and processes that are rarely at the center of policy discussions. Indeed, much that he advocated would require dramatic shifts in school organization, in pedagogic practice, and, most important, in teachers' and students' understanding of the aims of education.

Dewey supported curricular activities that helped turn schools into "a genuine form of active community life, instead of a place set apart in which to learn lessons" ([1900] 1956, 14). By engaging students in life's actual tasks (gardening, building a structure, running a business, evaluating a social policy), he hoped to mirror the social and interdependent nature of the broader community.

The experience-based model put forward by Eliot Wigginton (1986) may help to clarify this approach. While producing *Foxfire* (a periodical that chronicles and reflects on life in Appalachia), students must work together on design, writing, editing, and production. These activities teach students how to work toward common ends at the same time that they demonstrate that the ability to pursue particular goals depends on social organization and a willingness to consider divergent perspectives. These experiences also provide an opportunity for a group to build on the different academic and nonacademic talents of its members and to model the use of these talents for social purposes. Dewey would not worry if students had different experiences. He felt that "efficiency in production often demands division of labor" ([1916] 1966, 85). However, he would worry if opportunities were divided in exploitative ways that alienated the participants from the purpose of their endeavor.

For a related set of reasons, Dewey supported activities in which students interacted within their home community or neighborhood (see Dewey, 1915; also see Newmann and Oliver, 1967). This emphasis on neighborly community, however, did not lead him to advocate exclusivity or isolation. Although he championed the importance of local community, he did not support attempts by subgroups within the community to create either homogeneous or elitist school environments. Dewey feared that isolation and exclusiveness made "for rigidity and formal institutionalizing of life, for static and selfish ideals within the group" ([1916] 1966, 86). His belief that growth required exposure to other perspectives led him to emphasize the importance of critics and the need to protect divergent voices.

Dewey's commitment to connecting subject matter to students' life experiences stems also from his belief that this approach afforded students a clearer understanding of the subject at hand. Desirable activities do more than bring students together; they also build on prior experiences and expand students' understanding of important areas of study. Dewey downplayed neither the importance of subject-matter knowledge nor the need to study this information in a coherent and orderly manner. He did, however, emphasize the need to place the path to that knowledge in students' individual and collective interests and experiences (see Dewey, [1938] 1963, chapter 7).

Dewey also criticized harshly the entrenched and pervasive individual and competitive aspects of schooling. He worried that this orientation might prevent students from developing a sense of connection and obligation to one another. Such systems also might promote egoism, isolation, selfishness, and destructive forms of competition. He points out that

> the mere absorbing of facts and truths is so exclusively individual an affair that it tends very naturally to pass into selfishness. There is no obvious social mode noted for the acquirement of mere learning. . . . Indeed, almost the only measure for success is a competitive one, in the bad sense of that term . . . so thoroughly is this the prevailing atmosphere that for one child to help another in his task has become a school crime. ([1900] 1956, 15–16)

Moreover, when the prime motivation for educational excellence is economic prosperity and when schools serve as a mechanism for sorting students, the educational process diminishes rather than fosters community. When schools sort students, they make one child's success dependent on another's failure. Such competition weakens the social bond because it teaches students to attend to personal interests rather than social needs.

This is not to say that the schools fail to train students in ways that foster economic productivity. Dewey does not worry that the schools are ineffective. What troubles him are their effects. We turn out "efficient industrial fodder" and "citizenship fodder" (1930, 127), but we fail to engage students in critical inquiries in which they identify, debate, and respond to the needs of our society.

Democratic Communitarians and Rights Theorists

Dewey's attention to the educational process and his rejection of material productivity make clear his differences with policy analysts who adopt a utilitarian focus on human capital development. Less striking are the differences between democratic communitarians and rights theorists. Rights theorists often argue that their model is fully capable of appreciating and fostering community. They believe that desirable communities can be built through voluntary association of individuals with shared values. "Collective activity," Rawls (1971) writes,

> is the preeminent form of human flourishing. For given favorable conditions, it is by maintaining these public arrangements that persons best express their nature and achieve the widest regulative excellences of which each is capable. At the same time just institutions allow for and encourage the diverse internal life of associations in which individuals realize their more particular aims. (529)

> The main idea is simply that a well-ordered society (corresponding to justice as fairness) is itself a form of social union. Indeed, it is a social union of social unions. (527)

Similarly, some rights theorists who do not accept the primacy of communitarian ethics do nonetheless believe that attention to communitarian goals can improve upon a liberal social order. Amy Gutmann (1985) believes that communitarian arguments highlight important concerns. They can "supplement" though not "supplant" basic liberal values (320).[5]

These rights theorists doubt neither the impact of community nor the potential desirability of community. When assessing social institutions, however, their first priority is justice, not community. It is this stance that Dewey criticizes. Dewey puts community first.

Dewey would not say it like this, of course. Hating dualisms as he did, he would likely argue that we must develop understandings of justice that fit our conceptions of a democratic community. It is interesting, however, that he does not emphasize concern for justice. Indeed, the term "justice" does not even appear in the index to *Democracy and Education*. (Similarly, although Rawls, 1971, uses the term "democratic equality" to describe his ideal form of justice, he does not directly discuss the meaning of democracy or include that term in his index.) The important point is that while Dewey would recognize value in many liberal visions of justice, his commitment to community would take precedence. The consequences of this ordering become clearer when one examines his understanding of freedom and equality.

Freedom Within Community. Both utilitarians and rights theorists emphasize the importance of freeing individuals so that they can choose their own conception of "the good." To the extent possible, they want policy makers to remain neutral with respect to this choice.[6] Dewey, in contrast, puts forward a communitarian vision of freedom. He argues that social forces shape the goals individuals "choose" to pursue and that social organization often enables their pursuit. Dewey worries that educators who, following Rousseau's vision in *Émile*, emphasize the importance of "free" development fail to appreciate the degree to which children's environments and previous experiences direct their growth. "Free" students do not always learn and grow in desirable ways.[7]

Dewey's desire to direct individual growth did not diminish the importance he placed on freedom as a goal, but it did lead him to argue that liberal notions linking freedom to autonomy were problematic. Those following "the official creed of historic liberalism," Dewey wrote, prize a generalized conception of freedom "at the expense of positive abilities" (1922, 210).[8] This traditional liberal perspective emphasizes the connection between autonomy and freedom and obscures the ways in which social organization can foster greater individual freedom. Collective efforts can create the infrastructure and supply the support that enables individuals to pursue valued goals. Freedom is often a social achievement, the product of organization and collective effort. Just as one's freedom to drive expands when the society organizes a system of roads, a student's freedom to identify, examine, and respond to significant academic and social issues often demands collective commitments to analysis and action.

Such social organization generally requires constraints on individual autonomy. Thus, while democratic communitarians hope to promote educational practices that respect the varied interests and abilities of students, they also expect students to participate in collective efforts that do not always align with their personal preferences.

This perspective has considerable implications for curriculum, pedagogy, and school organization. Rather than focusing on the liberal goals of "autonomous" growth and neutrality with respect to different visions of the good, democratic communitarians emphasize the transformative potential of the educational enterprise. They want educators to direct student interests, aptitudes, and skills toward social ends and what they view as desirable social processes. More specifically, they want educators to modify social forces by creating educational experiences that lead students to make "choices" that are informed by a democratic process—one that attends to students' interests, their abilities, scientific study, and the community's needs and priorities.

In addition to strengthening bonds among students, these collective experiences model desirable modes of association. In the laboratory school at the University of Chicago, for example, the occupational settings Dewey designed for students reflected the industrial world he hoped to create, not the one that existed at the time. Students worked together in cooperative communities. The power and privilege of management was constrained. Workers helped choose both their goals and strategies for meeting those goals (see Westbrook, 1991, 1992).

Equity Within Community. Dewey's discussion of educational equality also highlights his differences with mainstream educators committed to justice. Mainstream educators emphasize equality of opportunity and equality of outcome. They aim to equalize educational inputs (school conditions, class size finances, curriculum) so that individual students compete on a level playing field. They also support compensatory educational strategies (Head Start, smaller classes, counseling) for disadvantaged students that aim to equalize educational outcomes (generally measured by standardized test scores). More complex forms of equality are certainly imaginable, but it is this kind of bureaucratic equality, with an emphasis on direct comparisons of specified inputs and outputs, that generally receives educational policy analysts' attention.

Dewey supports neither uniform pedagogy nor standardized educational goals. The diversity of students' needs, interest, and experiences, he argues, makes uniform treatment inappropriate. Dewey also worries that educators' efforts to equalize student performance lead them to adopt standardized measures of educational achievement that channel student energies toward narrow and predefined academic and vocational goals. This process prevents fulfillment of individual potentialities. When Dewey wrote, "What the best and wisest parent wants for his own child, that must the community want for all of its children," he was not arguing that all students should receive a standardized education. He was proclaiming the need to attend to "the full growth of all individuals" ([1900] 1956, 7).

Dewey wants educational policy to respond to social and economic inequalities, but unlike mainstream proponents of equality, he neither holds the same goals for all students nor recommends that all students receive the same pedagogic and curricular approaches. Instead, he argues:

> School facilities must be secured of such amplitude and efficiency as will in fact and not simply in name discount the effects of economic inequalities. . . . Accomplishment of this end demands not only adequate administrative provision of school facilities, and such supplementation of family resources as will enable youth to take advantage of them, *but also such modification of traditional ideals of culture, traditional subjects of study and traditional methods of teaching and discipline* as will retain all the youth under educational influences until they are equipped to be masters of their own economic and social careers. ([1916] 1966, 98, emphasis added)

Standardized notions of equality also may weaken social bonds. Uniform and comparative measures of success can transform notions of opportunity and achievement into zero-sum arrangements. This occurs when a student's grade in a class or score on a standardized test reflects his or her achievement relative to others and not any prespecified standard. As a consequence, the success of some students comes to depend on the failure of others. Such systems may foster destructive forms of competition and undermine the development of supportive community relationships. In fact, as students get older, studies show that they increasingly come to view themselves as successful at a given task only when they perform that task better than others (see Nicholls, 1989).

This example helps explain democratic communitarians' desire to modify calls for equality. Mainstream rhetoric connecting "equal opportunity" with "democracy" often neglects a crucial third ingredient—community. As Tocqueville explained well over a century ago, the quest for equality among those who lack community is problematic. It leaves unfulfilled the dreams inspired by equality of opportunity and can make individuals barriers to one another's success:

> The same equality which allows each man to entertain vast hopes makes each man by himself weak. . . . Not only are men powerless by themselves, but at every step they find immense obstacles which they had not at first noticed. They have abolished the troublesome privileges of some of their fellows, but they come up against the competition of all. The barrier has changed shape rather than place. (Tocqueville, [1848] 1966, 537; see also Dewey, 1927, 149–50)

This reasoning would lead democratic communitarians to argue that educators who focus on providing meritocratic environments have misdiagnosed the central problem—or at least ignored one of its most challenging components. The need is for settings in which equal opportunity and community are pursued simultaneously. These educational experiences might lead to identification of students with particular abilities, but they would not be designed to sort students in an equitable manner.

Justice as a Remedial Virtue

Sandel's (1982) discussion of the limits of liberalism may help to summarize the difference between liberal and communitarian priorities. Sandel views justice as a remedial virtue. While justice is an adequate remedy for injustice, he rejects Rawls's (1971) claim that it "is the first principle for social institutions" (3). When policy makers begin with a focus on justice, Sandel argues that they miss opportunities to promote or sustain higher and more desirable arrangements built on mutual commitment, group consensus, and supportive community. When the focus is on justice, social bonds become optional, a function of expediency, rather than the desirable end. For these reasons, Sandel believes that the need to resort to fairness and equality signifies a decreased expectation. For Sandel, relations that mirror those of an ideal family are more desirable than relationships governed by a commitment to justice. In ideal families decisions reflect "spontaneous affection," love, and a sense of mutual commitment rather than a commitment to fairness.

The implications for educational policy analysis are substantial. Dewey would agree with Sandel's claim that while justice is preferable to injustice, it should not guide the aims or practices of educational institutions. Mainstream policy analysts' pursuit of just educational strategies may lead educators to teach cognitive skills in an equitable and efficient manner. However, this focus also may reinforce and legitimize narrow understandings of self-interest, notions of individual autonomy, and destructive forms of competition. These orientations threaten social bonds and reduce our chances for democratic community. Moreover, a commitment to liberal notions of justice can constrain the ability of educational institutions to transform students' character in ways that make democratic communities more likely. Commitments to individual liberty may also prevent educators from designing curriculum and pedagogy so as to foster particular attitudes with respect to interpersonal obligations, the importance of social goals, and group decision-making processes.

Communitarian Schools Within a Liberal Democratic Society

Michael Sandel's model of an ideal family seems an unrealistic goal for an entire society. Indeed, it would be quite dangerous to pursue social institutions in which the state could make the kind of profound claims upon individuals that family members make upon each other. Ideal families are just that—ideal. Historical experiences with totalitarian governments should suggest caution for those who pose romantic visions of social institutions operating like families.

Still, it is significant that Dewey ([1900] 1956) references "what the best and wisest parent wants for his own child" (7) when creating the standard that should determine the community's educational policies and practices. He rejects the idea that abstract notions of "freedom" or "justice" should be the standard. It is the ideal parent that can make contextually appropriate decisions.

Some also might argue that Dewey's democratic communitarian vision is that of a romantic. The diversity and constant change of modern society make it difficult to foster the sense of shared aims and the commitment to democratic processes needed to govern major social institutions in accordance with democratic communitarian values. As Gutmann (1985) writes, "Justice need not be the only virtue of social institutions for it to be better than anything we are capable of putting in its place" (322). Indeed, the point of this discussion is not so much to advocate the superiority of democratic communitarian values over justice. Rather, it is to note the value of including systematic attention to democratic communitarian ideals along with the focus on equity and justice.

For those hoping to infuse society with democratic communitarian values, schools may be a particularly good place to start. Schools with this goal might provide students much needed access to the kind of support, sense of connection, and direction that help make lives meaningful, productive, and pleasant. These schools also might provide a vision and set of experiences that diminish the alienation, narrow understanding of self-interest, and destructive competition that pervade the broader community.

Current policy analysis diminishes this possibility. Assessment of educational quality reflects an emphasis on individual rather than group achievement, standardized and competitive notions of equality, and narrow monetary understandings of utility. Evaluators and policy analysts assess the achievement of individual students working on their own. They do not ask how well a class or group of students can work together toward a common goal. Similarly, they choose not to assess the degree to which schools pass on to students a "framework of group obligation," the capacity to care for one another, or a commitment to assessing and responding to their community's needs. More generally, evaluators and policy analysts rarely focus on the transformative power of education. Despite the respect Dewey commands, those assessing educational policy generally do not emphasize the social concerns of democratic communitarians.

4
Humanistic Psychology

The importance of "helping children to realize their full potential," "educating the whole child," and "tailoring education to the distinct needs of individual children" are frequently proclaimed in educational policy rhetoric. However, while policy discussions often highlight these goals of humanistic psychology, they rarely make them the subject of systematic study. Like a sign proclaiming, "the customer always comes first," analysts' rhetorical commitments to fully developing students' potential seem more a cultural trademark than a manifestation of an actual policy goal.

In contrast, behaviorist and neo-behaviorist psychological theories do receive considerable attention from the educational policy community. Research by these psychologists has helped to shape mainstream educational perspectives on testing, motivation, and numerous other aspects of learning theory. This work has not, however, generally engaged ethical concerns. Behaviorists and neo-behaviorists tend to pursue a utilitarian agenda and to focus on technical issues. Adopting a scientific orientation, they aim for social efficiency and for engineering particular outcomes. They focus, for example, on increasing test scores, measures of motivation, and personal agency beliefs. They have been relatively silent during discussions of ethical priorities. As Abraham Maslow (1968a) has noted:

> Classical academic psychology has no systematic place for higher-order elements of the personality such as altruism and dignity, or the search for truth and beauty. You simply do not ask questions about ultimate human values if you are working in an animal lab. (686)

Humanistic psychologists directly engage these value-laden considerations. In this chapter, I focus specifically on the humanistic theories of the 1960s and 1970s and principally on the work of Abraham Maslow and Carl Rogers. These theorists put forward a synthesis of the psychological and existential theories of Freud, Adler, Jung, Fromm, and others. Their model provides an alternative to classical academic psychology that emphasizes scientific study of behavior and

Freudian psychologies used by both clinical psychologists and social workers. This psychologically based ethical system employs counseling, education, and attention to basic human needs to help individuals strive toward realization of their potential. Self-actualization (the full realization of an individual's potential) is the ultimate goal.

The growth of this movement coincided with counterculture movements ("encounter groups" and "human growth centers," for example, as typified by the Esalen Institute at Big Sur in California) that ultimately shaped and in many ways distorted humanistic theory. My focus here is on the earlier position as articulated by Abraham Maslow, Carl Rogers, and others (see Smith, 1990).

THE CENTRAL COMMITMENTS OF HUMANISTIC PSYCHOLOGY

Humanistic psychology attends to a full range of human capacities. It emphasizes the need to uncover an individual's true nature, to respond to existential dilemmas, and to improve the quality of an individual's personal and professional relations.

Maslow's ultimate goal, self-actualization, represents the full development of an individual's intrinsic nature, talents, and capacities. This perspective carries with it four central commitments. First, Maslow borrows from Nietzsche's notion of an individual will freed from the distortions imposed by societal pressures. Maslow speaks of "striving toward health, the quest for identity and autonomy, the yearning for excellence . . . " (1970, xii) and, more generally, of the need to pursue one's true nature. Second, he argues for the importance of fully developing a broad range of social, cognitive, and affective traits that he associates with full human development. This commitment makes his approach substantially different from that of many utilitarian and rights-oriented educational policy analysts who focus on the development of human capital. Third, Maslow argues that self-actualization requires attention to a hierarchy of innate human needs that he feels are a prerequisite for self-actualization. These needs include (1) physiological needs (food, water, sleep, and exercise); (2) safety and security needs (freedom from fear, physical violence, and abuse); (3) love and belonging needs (needs for friendship, love, and a sense of rootedness); (4) self-esteem needs (positive self-concept and respect from others) (see Farmer, 1984, 163–64). Finally, Maslow endorses a romanticized conception of natural human development, which in many ways is consistent with Rousseau's. He believes that children, when freed from the conventions and pressures of modern society, will develop positive traits and more fully realize their potentials.

HUMANISTIC PSYCHOLOGY AND EDUCATIONAL POLICY

These four principles also can be used to frame the agenda of humanistic educators (see Farmer, 1984). First, humanistic educators strive to create educational settings in which children can pursue and develop their true nature. For Maslow, education is a kind of therapy that helps individuals identify and pursue their own natural inclinations: "The job of the psychotherapist (or the teacher) is to help a person find out what's already in him [*sic*] rather than to reinforce him or shape or teach him into a prearranged form" (1968a, 688). Pursuit of what he calls an individual's "instinctoid nature" requires that a person strip away the influences of cultural experiences in order to locate his or her distinct needs and proclivities. To accomplish this goal, students enter a somewhat therapeutic relationship with a teacher or counselor. In addition, Maslow believes that examination of one's reaction to peak experiences, "experiences which give rise to love, hate, anxiety, depression, and joy" (McNeil, 1985, 6), can help each individual student identify a "real self" (Maslow, 1968a, 688; see Maslow, 1968b, for examples). Such experiences are therefore a central component of his educational plan.

Second, psychological humanists hope to facilitate educational experiences that promote development of a broad range of social, cognitive, and affective qualities. They reject a perspective, common among educational policy analysts, that frames the purpose of education primarily in terms of cognitive growth. Rather than focusing on what Rogers (1983) refers to as "education from the neck up" (19), humanistic educators attend to a wide range of concerns. Is a given student comfortable and competent at work, in social settings, and in personal relationships? Has the student had opportunities to explore creative outlets, athletic challenges, and academic endeavors? Is the student happy? Are his or her relations with friends and family desirable? The "whole child"—his or her cognitive, affective, and physical well-being—must receive attention.

These commitments lead humanists to value a wide range of educational experiences. They might even support the cooperative educational activities that communitarians value, because such activities provide students opportunities to develop their interpersonal skills.

However, unlike communitarians, they would not design collective activities that lead students to adopt the group's goals as their own. Instead of trying to help students identify a shared set of goals for the community, humanistic educators want students to identify and pursue their own unique and broadly conceived interests and needs.

Third, humanistically oriented educators attend to the four innate or basic needs of individuals. According to humanistic theory, physiological needs, safety and security needs, love and belonging needs, and self-esteem needs must be satisfied before students can move toward self-actualization. A focus on these priorities would lead educational analysts to attend to a broad range of concerns. Are students eating well? Do schools offer them a sense of respect and opportunities for success? Do students feel both physically safe and comfortable expressing their opinions?

Humanists would worry about reports that indicate that many schools are overcrowded, impersonal, and dangerous. They would demand action in response to Justice Department statistics that indicate that roughly 100,000 students bring guns to school on any particular day (De Witt, 1993). As Jonathan Kozol (1991) and others make clear, many schools fail to meet what humanists regard as children's basic needs. These shortcomings are not limited to urban or poor rural schools. Even, and some would argue often, in wealthy communities and at the nation's best endowed private schools, many children grow up in environments that fail to support healthy growth (see Crosier, 1991).

The public does not ignore these concerns for basic needs, but mainstream educators rarely make them the subject of methodical analysis. Often, when these issues are raised their significance is linked to poor academic performance. "Fear for their personal safety impedes learning for far too many New York City students," write the editors of the *New York Times* (1993, A14). Unlike mainstream analysts who write that we must meet children's basic needs if we are to reduce their risk of failure, humanists would write that inadequately meeting these needs constitutes failure.

Finally, psychological humanists strive to create an educational environment in which children are "free to learn." They emphasize both the process and the product of education and subscribe to the notion that free individuals will embark on a course of studies that is both natural and desirable. Teachers can facilitate the creation of learning opportunities by permitting students to follow the direction of their desires and interests. As Carl Rogers (1983) explains:

> [Significant learning] has a quality of personal involvement. . . . It is self-initiated. Even when the impetus or stimulus comes from the outside, the sense of discovery, of reaching out, of grasping and comprehending, comes from within. It is pervasive. It makes a difference in the behavior, attitudes, perhaps even the personality of the learner. She knows whether it is meeting her need, whether it leads toward what she wants to know, whether it illuminates the dark area of ignorance she is experiencing. (20)

Electives and independent studies are consistent with this priority. In addition, humanistic educators would be hesitant to accept national or state-mandated curriculum frameworks, fearing that such policy might lead to standardized rather than individually tailored educational experiences.

CONNECTING HUMANISTIC PSYCHOLOGY TO PROMINENT SCHOOLS OF PHILOSOPHICAL AND EDUCATIONAL THOUGHT

In some important respects it seems inappropriate to place humanistic psychologists' theories of self-actualization side by side with theories of utility, individual rights, and democratic community. Bentham, Mill, Rawls, and Dewey are central figures in Western philosophy. The psychological theories of Maslow and Rogers, especially when viewed from the standpoint of educational philosophy, are more a short-lived manifestation of a particular branch of progressive ideology than a distinct school of thought. Humanistic psychology reflects a constellation of beliefs about human nature and human development, but fails to offer a clear theory linking schools and society. Why include this framework?

From the standpoint of this study, the attraction of humanistic psychology stems from its individualistic orientation, its strong historical ties to other prominent educational visions, the model's relative simplicity, and the broad-based popular support it engenders.

First, as Alasdair MacIntyre (1981) makes clear in his influential critique of post-Enlightenment theories of utility and justice, there are two primary alternatives to mainstream theories of utility and rights. One can, as he recommends, focus on developing communities that pursue an Aristotelian ideal and emphasize the harmonious alignment of the state and the citizen. Alternatively, one can endorse Nietzsche's radical proposal that individuals reject the constraints of social institutions and seek to live in accordance with their true natures. Thus, if communitarian thought provides one option for those who question policy analysts' nearly exclusive focus on maximizing individual utility and projecting individual rights, humanistic psychology provides another. In fact, Maslow borrows from Nietzsche when defining self-actualization. He writes that self-actualization is "the use and exploitation of talents, capacities, potentialities, etc. . . . reminding us of Nietzsche's exhortation, 'Become what thou art!'" (Maslow, 1954, 200–1). Nietzsche believed that the forces of culture, the state, and the church constrain and distort our individuality. He felt that each individual must work to transcend these forces and the personal values they create and must adhere to his or her true nature and inclinations. These themes are central tenets of humanistic psychology. Furthermore, this emphasis on developing each individual's true nature differs significantly from the goals embedded in policy analysts' understandings of individual utility and rights.

While recognizing these ties to Nietzsche's vision, however, I do not wish to overstate the case. Nietzsche rejected the romantic notion (often embedded in the writings of humanistic psychologists) that an individual's pursuit of self-actualization would be socially desirable or viewed positively by others. Indeed, since Nietzsche's form of self-actualization requires rejection of traditional values, including reason and morality, it seems unlikely that most humanistic psychologists would view this result positively or that they would assist individuals who seek this transformation. Moreover, for the individuals involved, this process might well be painful (see Rosenow, 1989; Hillesheim, 1986).

While the alignment of humanistic psychology with Nietzsche's philosophy is relatively weak, the parallels between humanistic perspectives and progressive educational thought are a good bit stronger. Humanistic psychology represents a modern manifestation of the romantic, individualistic, progressive ideal.

Much that Rousseau wrote, for example, aligns with notions of self-actualization. Prior to the creation of civil society, Rousseau hypothesized that individuals lived spontaneously, instinctively, and happily in nature. They attended to their own needs and were guided by *amour de soi* (which can be translated as "self-love"). The force of *amour de soi* guided behavior in accordance with the natural order. Living in this state of nature, people were self-actualized. Rousseau went on to argue that the instinctive motivational forces that served individuals well in the first state of nature had less desirable implications for individuals living in a civil society.

His concerns were similar to those of humanistic psychologists. He worried that educating men[1] in response to the priorities of the society would lead to the use of incentives (rewards and punishments) that were not connected to a natural learning process. Such practices would teach students the art of manipulation and would foster envy, competition, and pride rather than furthering their natural and desirable growth. These traits were undesirable both because they led to a kind of selfishness that promoted needless suffering and because they shifted attention away from full human development and toward narrow materialistic goals. Thus, Rousseau shared humanistic psychologists' concern that the norms, values, and incentives of modern societies often distorted and polluted the natural process of growth. Furthermore, Rousseau, like humanistic psychologists, expressed confidence in the desirability of development freed from societal influence.

Rousseau also emphasized the importance of aligning educational experiences with the child's developmental process. This stance sharply differed from the prevailing educational beliefs of his day, which held that students should be socialized to adopt both the skills and the social habits they would need as adults. Articulating values that humanistic psychologists hold dear, Rousseau wrote:

> Nature would have children be children before they are men. If we try to invert this order we shall produce a forced fruit, immature and flavorless, fruit that rots before it can ripen. . . . Childhood has its own ways of thinking, seeing, and feeling. (in Dewey, 1915, 7)

Finally, Rousseau was committed to developing a full range of human potentials. He shared with modern humanists the belief that educators commonly neglect many aspects of healthy development. Maslow, Rogers, and other humanistic psychologists would likely agree with his educational plan for Emile, "life is the business I would have him learn" (Rousseau, [1762] 1956, 15).[2]

The alignment of humanistic psychology with progressive educational thought does not end with Rousseau. Dewey, of course, also placed enormous emphasis on the need to align educational opportunities with students' inclinations and desires. Moreover, his work did much to inspire the emphasis that progressive and humanistic educators place on promoting personal and social development along with academic development. Indeed, these priorities represent a recurring theme throughout the past century. They are evident, for example, in many of the principles put forward by the Progressive Education Association in 1930:

1. "The Child's Physical Well Being ... The school should observe closely the physical condition of each pupil, and in cooperation with the home make abundant health available to every child."
2. "Opportunity for Full Development. Opportunity for initiative and self-expression should be provided in an environment rich in interesting material."
3. "Social Development and Discipline ... Discipline should be a matter of self-mastery rather than external compulsion."
4. "The Curriculum. The Curriculum should be based on the nature and needs of childhood and youth" (Progressive Education Association, 1930, 1).

Thus, humanistic psychology embodies themes that have long been central concerns of educators. Moreover, this perspective's relatively straightforward formulation, explicit description of goals, and widespread popular support make it an attractive framework for policy analysts. Ironically, however, many of the same features that make this model relatively straightforward and popular among citizens, are also the subject of substantial criticism. Although this criticism highlights the need to bolster or modify humanistic psychological theory so that it can stand firmly on its own, it should not overshadow the theory's ability to help analysts locate problems in prevailing school policies and imagine new possibilities.

Some Concerns Regarding Humanistic Psychology

Critiques of Maslow and other theorists of self-actualization take a number of forms. First, both psychologists and philosophers have criticized Maslow's methodology. He appealed to his own personal conception of fully developed individuals when he selected his sample of self-actualized persons. As M. Brewster Smith (1969) points out, Maslow chose to focus not on Van Gogh or Lenin but instead on such figures as Jefferson, Einstein, and Jane Addams. Since Maslow determined the definition of psychological health by examining the qualities of those he admired most, his empirical understanding of self-actualization reflects his own value commitments. To the extent that readers hold similar values, his theory may still be of interest. However, Maslow's claim to a scientifically grounded foundation appears unreasonable. In addition, neither Maslow nor others who emphasized full realization of individual potential present evidence to justify the romantic view that without the interference of society individuals will develop in desirable ways. As Smith (1973) writes, "Vice and evil are as much in the range of human potentiality, I would argue, as virtue" (25; also see Scheffler, 1985).

Furthermore, Maslow's hierarchy of human needs may oversimplify a set of complex dynamics. There are numerous instances in which it fails to hold up. The need for food or shelter, for example, may be less if other, "higher-order needs" are being met. In addition, many individuals who lacked safety and other basic needs have made profound contributions to, for example, the arts and the cause of social justice. While attention to human needs is clearly warranted, the hierarchy he describes and the notion that satisfying these needs is a prerequisite for self-actualization seems questionable.

On a more fundamental level, humanistic psychologists are faulted for emphasizing discovery of an individual's "innate" nature. Philosophers point out that it is a mistake to speak of an individual's "true" nature as existing outside of social contexts:

> As a matter of fact every individual has grown up, and always must grow up, in a social medium. His responses grow intelligent, or gain meaning, simply because he lives and acts in a medium of accepted meanings and values. Through social intercourse, through sharing in the activities embodying beliefs, he gradually acquires a mind of his own. The conception of mind as a purely isolated possession of the self is at the very antipodes of the truth. (Dewey, [1916] 1966, 295)

Thus, Dewey rejects humanists' contention that "full realization of potential" has a meaning that transcends social contexts. This critique has a pedagogic corollary. Dewey would reject the beliefs and practices of many humanists and progressive educators who feel that educators must simply get out of the way and let students direct their own learning process. As he explains most clearly in *Experience and Education* ([1938] 1963), teachers must create learning environments that lead students to identify and engage in activities that foster personally and socially fulfilling growth among students.

Critics also point to the potentially conservative policy implications of humanistic psychology's focus on the individual (Bell and Schniedewind, 1989; Geller, 1982; Fantini, 1974). By focusing on individuals and on personal development rather than on society, humanists may obscure the significance of social institutions and the need for social justice. For example, humanists rarely talk about changing the factors in the social and economic environment that make it difficult for individuals to satisfy their basic needs or reach their full potential. Similarly, many higher order dysfunctions such as apathy, envy, jealousy, resignation, and despair plague individuals whose basic needs have been satisfied. These outcomes, critics charge, are products of societal and institutional arrangements that foster destructive competition, empty consumerism, and various status hierarchies. Humanists try to help individuals strip away the distorting and harmful impact of these social and economic forces, but they generally recommend therapy for individuals rather than institutional change. In response to this problem, Bell and Schniedewind (1989) argue that humanistic educators should modify their theory and create an approach to education that blends humanistic pedagogy with the analysis of social institutions fostered by critical theorists. For example, they describe a high school women's studies curriculum titled "Changing Learning: Changing Lives," which

> integrates the personal and the social by helping students build self-confidence and self-esteem; understand the inequities of the social system in regard to class, race, and sex, and see how these inequities affect them; and turn their anger away from themselves toward the institutions that oppress them. (215)

THE COMPATIBILITY OF SELF-ACTUALIZATION WITH THE FUNCTIONAL UTILITARIAN PERSPECTIVE

Concern for self-actualization often is portrayed as compatible with the functional utilitarian perspective. Clearly, the acquisition of cognitive and practical skills will help many to reach their full potential. Similarly, attention to students' unique interests, desires, and concerns often may help motivate students to achieve academically. However, analysis of what it would mean to educate in a manner consistent with the tenets of self-actualization calls into question the belief that many educators truly are pursuing both goals simultaneously. Maslow (1968a) makes this point when he states:

> I would maintain that a good 90% of "learning theory" deals with learnings that have nothing to do with . . . specieshood and biological idiosyncracy. This kind of learning too easily reflects the goals of the teacher and ignores the values and ends of the learner himself. It is also fair, therefore, to call such learning amoral. (691)

Pedagogic approaches in line with self-actualization differ substantially from educational practice guided by utilitarian concerns. Programs designed to promote self-actualization respond to individual proclivities, interests, and multiple aspects of students' personal development. Maslow (1968a) believed that "learning-to-be-a-person ... [should be of more importance to educators] than the impersonal learning of skills or the acquisition of habits" (692). Humanistic psychologists want to help students become what they are—not to enable their pursuit of utility.

In contrast, functional utilitarian educators view schooling as a means of fostering individual and collective productivity. They are hesitant to permit students' desires and inclinations to structure the style and content of students' educational experience. They might try to respond to student interests if it helps them teach math or reading skills. But, if an alternative approach, such as rewards and sanctions based on students' comparative ranking, works better as a motivator, then that approach would be used. Therefore, although humanistic psychologists and utilitarians might endorse some similar educational policies, they would do so for distinctly different reasons.

THE COMPATIBILITY OF HUMANISTIC PSYCHOLOGY WITH RIGHTS-ORIENTED PERSPECTIVES

Rights theorists and humanistic psychologists share many important ethical assumptions. Both make the individual the fundamental unit of analysis and respond to the significance of communities in similar ways. Each recognizes the influence of communities on individuals and the need for individuals to be affirmed by communities, and both worry that pressures of communities may constrain individual liberty and the free development of individual tastes. Indeed, one could make a strong case that humanistic psychology is actually a psychologically oriented version of liberal rights theory: one that relies on psychological notions of individual development rather than on economic modeling. After all, rights theorists as different in outlook as Nozick and Rawls would accept many of the assumptions and goals put forward by humanistic psychologists.

However, I would argue that humanistic psychology and rights orientations differ in a number of ways that are of particular relevance to educators. First, for reasons stated above, many rights theorists would be uncomfortable with the methodological approach used by Maslow and other humanistic psychologists to define the qualities of self-actualized individuals. Second, rights theorists would question humanists' conception of a desirable educational program. Most rights theorists define the aims of education rather narrowly. They want to ensure that a child's access to educational opportunities for cognitive growth align with various principles of justice, and they want educational policies that strengthen a student's abilities to rationally guide his or her own life. Finally, few rights theorists recommend that children be allowed to direct their own educational experiences. Rawls, for example, believes that a parent or teacher has the right to direct a child's educational experience in cases where the child is unable to rationally identify or pursue his or her goals (Rawls, 1971, 250; see also Gutmann, 1982).

In contrast to rights theorists, humanistic psychologists rarely discuss notions of justice or the way in which social institutions ought to structure access to educational opportunities. Instead they focus on ways educators can promote multiple aspects of personal development. They also support a therapeutic orientation toward education, which many rights theorists would hesitate to endorse.

HUMANISTIC PRIORITIES, CULTURAL VALUES, AND POLICY ANALYSIS

When educators talk about "helping students reach their full potential," "educating the whole child," or "tailoring education to the distinct needs of individual children," they are using the rhetoric of humanistic psychology. These humanistic commitments to individualism and excellence resonate powerfully within American culture. As a result, the introductions and conclusions of mainstream policy statements use rhetoric that aligns with the goals of these theorists. However, these bold pronouncements are rarely unpacked, examined, or translated into specific policies. The concerns of humanistic psychologists can help policy makers and policy analysts imagine and pursue an alternative set of educational ideals. At present, these remain marginal to mainstream policy analysis. Systematic consideration of humanistic priorities is rare.

5
Tracking

Between the mid-1980s and mid-1990s, literally hundreds of articles and reports have been written on tracking and ability grouping.[1] Dozens of books and dissertations focus on this subject as well. The desirability of different grouping strategies commonly is debated by teachers, school boards, parents, and academics.

The concept is hardly new. Plato argued that individuals should be sorted according to their ability, play a role in a hierarchical society determined by their ability, and receive an education that would prepare them for that destiny. The continuing interest in the topic stems from both the symbolic and the consequential nature of track assignments. This organizational feature of schools, perhaps more than any other, embodies commitments regarding the ends of education. For individual students, placement in a given track implies more than an educational plan—it implies a future. In addition, the kind of tracks we design and the methods we use to place students in them have social as well as educational significance.

For what kinds of careers are we preparing our children? Are all students receiving similar opportunities? To be sure, students will fulfill a range of roles in the society and the economy. Should their preparation therefore differ? If so, at what age should differentiation begin? Who should direct this process and on what should they base their decisions? Tracking structures say much about the world we expect and the one we hope to create.

With such matters at stake, it is not surprising that policy analysts often invoke the language and goals of utilitarians, rights theorists, democratic communitarians, and humanistic psychologists when discussing tracking policy. However, while the importance of community, democracy, and potential is affirmed in these discussions, the primary focus is on human capital development, utility, and equity. In fact, the visions of democracy, community, and human potential that analysts put forward are shaped in large part by more fundamental commitments to utilitarian and rights-oriented criteria.

EARLY DEBATES ON TRACKING

Since the expansion of public schooling around the turn of the century, the desirability of tracking as an organizational scheme has been hotly contested. Moreover, as Slavin (1990) explains, "arguments for and against ability grouping have been essentially similar for seventy years" (472). Those supporting both tracking and ability grouping have stressed the importance of aligning curriculum and pedagogy with student ability, of responding to students' academic and vocational needs, of connecting learning opportunities to merit, of reducing the failure and sense of failure experienced by low-achieving students, and of decreasing the demands placed on teachers.

Critics of ability-based tracking arrangements have charged that the practice stigmatizes students in low tracks, denies low-track students access to their more stimulating peers, cuts off opportunities for advancement, furthers a hierarchy based on class and race, and provides unequal educational experiences (for reviews see, for example, Slavin, 1990; Rosenbaum, 1980; Turney, 1931).

Opposition to Tracking by the National Education Association: The Committee of Ten Report

As the twentieth century began, school systems were expanding dramatically. High schools, previously populated by upper- and middle-class students, were coming to be seen as important for immigrants, day laborers, and others who previously had entered the work force at an early age (Tyack, 1974). Although the demand for more education was growing, consensus regarding its content had not been achieved. Some hoped to provide all students with a liberal education. They wanted a common high school curriculum that focused students' attention on Latin, English, math, history, geography, foreign languages, and the sciences. Others emphasized the importance of "social efficiency"—of aligning students' curriculum with what they would need to become productive workers.

Charles Eliot, the president of Harvard University, deserves careful attention because over the course of his career he moved from one camp to the other. Around the turn of the century, Eliot loudly proclaimed the importance of providing all secondary school students with a liberal education. In 1892, he chaired the National Education Association's Committee of Ten. The report this committee produced received tremendous attention—much of it negative. Particularly controversial was the notion that every subject which is taught at all in a secondary school should be taught in the same way and to the same extent to every pupil so long as he pursues it, no matter what the probable destination of the pupil may be, or at what point his education is to cease. (Eliot, [1894] 1961, 87)

Eliot believed that the vast majority of students could master an academic high school curriculum and that all students should be exposed to a liberal discipline-based education. He also rejected the idea that schools should sort young students in an effort to train them for particular occupations.

When justifying this stance Eliot appealed to utilitarian notions of efficiency. He also put forward a vision that appeared to focus on students' rights, democracy, and the free and full development of an individual's potential. More specifically, Eliot ([1905] 1961) believed that there was a most effective and efficient way to teach each subject and that teaching subjects in "three or four different ways . . . would inevitably be [wasteful]." Further, he believed that

> In democratic society the classification of pupils, according to their so-called probable destinations, should be postponed to the latest possible time of life [to keep options open]. . . . I have always believed that the individual child in a democratic society had a right to do his own prophesying about his own career. (Eliot, [1905] 1961, 152–53)

Eliot worried that if specialization occurred too early and if it was based on test results rather than on student ambitions and capacities, some students would be denied equal opportunity to achieve prized positions in the society. He also invoked the notion of democracy and a humanistic commitment to self-direction. However, as I will demonstrate later in this chapter, both Eliot and his critics pursued narrow understandings of these two goals—ones that emphasize utilitarian and rights-oriented concerns.

Educators' Rejection of the Arguments Against Tracking

Eliot's vision, although endorsed by the prestigious Committee of Ten, was ultimately rejected both by the public and by increasingly professional "progressive" educators. In fact, it was later rejected by Eliot himself. The response to the Committee's recommendations was threefold. Critics felt it was inefficient, elitist, and inequitable.

Those stressing efficiency believed that differentiation of teaching style and content permitted educators to align students' training with their needs and abilities. G. Stanley Hall (1904) wrote, for example, that the principle of uniformity "does not apply to the great army of incapables . . . for whose mental development heredity decrees a slow pace and early arrest, and for whom by general consent both studies and methods must be different" (510).

New measures of intelligence developed by Lewis Terman, Edward Thorndike, and others were used to buttress claims that individual ability and potential differed widely. Reformers hoped to use the science of testing to align curriculum with student capabilities to maximize efficiency. As Terman explained in his book *Intelligence Tests and School Reorganization,*

> Common sense tells us how necessary it is to take [intellectual] differences into account in the framing of curricula and methods, in the classification of children for instruction, and in their educational and vocational guidance. (in Chapman, 1988, 89)

Attempts to provide all students with a liberal education would sacrifice a valuable opportunity to tailor the pace and content of the class to student abilities and to provide less academically able students with much-needed vocational training.

The Committee of Ten's recommendation that all students receive a liberal education was criticized by progressive educators as elitist because it stressed preparation for college over vocational training. As Jurgen Herbst (1992) explains, "The committee members failed to acknowledge that they had made no provision for those students who sought prolonged schooling for other than disciplinary and academic purposes" (293). As Hall (1904) wrote at the time, "To fit for present entrance examinations involves an at least temporary unfitting for life. It is too sedentary, clerical, bookish [and] fail[s] to appeal to the best powers of youth" (513).

The Committee's recommendations were labeled inequitable because they ignored individual differences. In contrast, tying student placement to performance on measures of intelligence and ability—to merit—was both fair and appropriate. Oakes (1985) summarizes the history of these arguments for tracking as follows:

> Through the provision of different high school curricula, opportunities for success could be equalized by offering different groups of students programs suited to their backgrounds and probable futures. (32)

In short, the rationales used both to defend tracking and to create a single curriculum aligned with utilitarian and rights-oriented commitments to equity, excellence, and scientifically enabled efficiency. Moreover, a commitment to human capital development and general social efficiency ran throughout this rhetoric.

Narrow Understandings of Democracy and Human Potential

Language emphasizing human potential and democracy was commonly part of these discussions about tracking. The meanings discussants attached to the terms "human potential" and "democracy," however, differed in important ways from the understandings put forward by humanistic psychologists and democratic communitarians.

"Democracy." Although their differences were numerous, both advocates and critics of tracking used words that equated individual rights and meritocratic arrangements with democracy. Their disagreements centered on which organizational and curricular approaches would best provide students with a fair chance for advancement through education.[2]

Eliot worried that tracking procedures led to early vocational specialization in schools. This, he believed, threatened merit-based social mobility. "The transition from one [layer of society] to another must be kept easy. That is one of the fundamental principles of democratic society" (Eliot, 1909, 219).

Progressive proponents of tracking generally accepted Eliot's stance that democratic educational arrangements facilitated social mobility. Terman wanted transfers between tracks to be kept open since track placements based solely on intelligence tests would be "repugnant to American ideals of democracy" (in Chapman, 1988, 90).

Progressive reformers agreed with Eliot's emphasis on social mobility, but they disagreed with his position that differences in individual talents were relatively small. They rejected the claim that in relation "to the total number of school children, the incapables are always but an insignificant proportion" (Eliot, [1905] 1961, 154). Terman judged 80% of the immigrants he tested to be "feeble-minded." "Their dullness," he wrote, "seems to be racial, or at least in the family stocks from which they come" (in Oakes, 1985).

These students of psychology and testing believed that talents differed greatly. "To refuse this concession to the wide range of individual differences," Hall (1904) wrote in response to Eliot, "is a specious delusion." Indeed, blindness to individual differences threatened utility and efficiency as well as democracy:

In looking over the text-books for these two kinds of minds or "desti-
nations" [practical and professional], one is struck with the very limited amount of subject-matter which is common, and also with the
fact that . . . to force them into one mold would be wasteful, undemocratic, and pedagogically immoral. (Hall, 1904, 510–12)

This rights-based orientation to democracy differs substantially
from democratic communitarian understandings of democracy. Although democratic communitarian assessments of tracking will receive more detailed attention after recent tracking discussions are assessed, it makes sense to point out here some of the ways democratic
communitarian analysts might criticize the narrow understanding of
democracy put forward by mainstream analysts.

First, the elites who debated the desirability of tracking assumed
that their goals accurately represented the priorities both of individual
students and of the society at large. Their rhetoric implied a commitment to the community's needs. For example, when laying down the
Cardinal Principles of Secondary Education, they wrote that "secondary
education should be determined by the needs of the society to be
served" (Department of the Interior, [1918] 1928, 1). However, when
they identified these needs and ways schools could respond, their priorities were often shaped by tradition (e.g., Eliot wanted all to receive
a traditional "liberal" education) and by their perspectives as societal
elites rather than by democratic deliberation. This notion that a natural
aristocracy of experts should guide educational policy also was reflected in the educational goals they pursued. Rather than emphasizing critical thinking or preparing students to be active participants in
policy discussions, Eliot, for example, hoped schools would teach students to "respect and confide in the expert in every field of human
activity" (in Preskill, 1989, 356).

Democratic communitarians also would be troubled by conclusions these experts reached. They would be frustrated that progressive
analysts and policy makers used their commitment to democracy to
justify the creation of vocational programs designed to fit students into
predetermined and hierarchically arranged roles based on jobs, roles
assumed class divisions and thereby constrained individual and social
growth. Lewis Terman wrote, for example, that low-ability children
"should be segregated in special classes. . . . They cannot master ab-
stractions, but they can often be made efficient workers" (in Bowles
and Gintis, 1976, 123).

Dewey ([1916] 1966) traces this problematic orientation to Plato,
who put forward "a limited number of classes of capacities and social

arrangements" (88). Despite Dewey's argument against this traditional perspective, however, it was adopted by most who discussed the pros and cons of tracking. Elwood P. Cubberley, for example, forcefully proclaimed the concern for social efficiency and for a fixed social hierarchy that led many to endorse tracking.

> Our city schools will soon be forced to give up the exceedingly democratic idea that all are equal, and our society devoid of classes . . . and to begin a specialization of educational effort along many lines in an attempt to adapt the school to the needs of the many classes. (Cubberley, 1909, 56–57)

Even Eliot, who is praised by many (see, for example, Oakes, 1985; Ravitch, 1985) for his opposition to tracking and his emphasis on equal and universal exposure to a liberal education, adopted a class-based model.

> What we need to appreciate and act upon in our democracy is the great fact that democratic society is divided, and is going to be divided into layers whose borders blend, whose limits are easily passed by individuals, but which, nevertheless, have distinct characteristics and distinct educational needs. (Eliot, 1909, 217)[3]

Indeed, in the first years of the twentieth century, as immigration continued to soar, Eliot's position came closer and closer to that of Hall, Terman, and the other champions of social efficiency. As Stephen Preskill (1989) so convincingly demonstrates, Eliot became a strong supporter of vocational education for blacks and for southern European immigrants, whom he regarded as genetically inferior. In 1908, he complained, for example, that the "immense majority of our children do not receive from our school system an education which trains them for the vocation to which they are clearly destined" (in Preskill, 1989, p. 356).

In general, then, both advocates and critics of tracking focused on meritocracy, which they equated with democracy. Their rhetoric mentions neither the importance of the public's participation in policy deliberation nor the need to fight hierarchies that can constrain the democratic process. In addition, little, if any, attention was paid to the impact of tracking on the kinds of communities that develop in schools or on pedagogic and curricular concerns of democratic communitarians.

Human Potential. There is much in the rhetoric of these debates that aligns with humanistic values. One group wanted to let a student "do his own prophesying about his own career" (Eliot, [1905] 1961, 153). They wanted to let students choose electives and to offer students an opportunity to choose among programs that emphasized different academic priorities (classical, Latin-scientific, modern languages, English). The other group of reformers emphasized "the enormous individual differences in intelligence which obtain from any unselected group of children" (Terman, 1920, 20). They stressed the importance of providing a variety of school programs tailored to students' capacities and interests through which students could reach their full potential.

To suggest, however, that either of these two groups was dedicated to humanistic values is to fall victim to their seductive rhetoric and to neglect their substantive commitments. In both cases, narrow notions of potential were put forward. Indeed, if a rights-based emphasis on equality and meritocracy shaped these educational leaders' use of the term "democracy," utilitarian concerns for human capital and cognitive development shaped their understanding of "human potential."

Eliot and the Committee of Ten, for example, stressed the importance of self-determination. The freedom they accorded students, however, was such that students were free to choose from various academic goals—not free to select or design an educational plan. Humanistic psychologists, in contrast, want to prepare students for full lives, while also attending to the quality of life they experience as students. Humanistic psychologists worry that educators' excessive focus on cognitive development constrains and distorts other aspects of growth. They would fault the substance of the Committee's plan on the grounds that it equates preparation for college with preparation for life. As Herbst (1992) points out:

> There was precious little evidence that committee members had ever considered seriously the question of how to prepare for life those who did not respond to academic training and mental discipline. (294)

Finally, the committee's plan would be criticized by humanists for its emphasis on uniform and teacher-centered pedagogy and curriculum. The committee, after all, argued that "for all pupils who study Latin, or history, or algebra, for example, the allotment of time, the method of instruction in a given school, [and the curricular content][4] should be [the same]" (Eliot, [1894] 1961, 87).[5]

Concern for the full development of individuals also would lead humanists to be critical of tracking proponents' plans and rationales. First, they would criticize the tests used by these scientists to assess potential on the grounds that they measured only a small range of talents. Second, humanists would object to the way these tests were used. The tests did not help individuals uncover their interests, but rather served to sort students. The tracks that were developed had narrow vocational orientations. These analysts equated human capital development with individual growth and human potential. Although these tracks may have prepared students for jobs, humanists would argue that they did not prepare students for life.[6]

Finally, although reformers spoke of tailoring instruction to individual proclivities, their tracks were hardly individualized. Instead, educators placed students in large groups and then provided them a uniform experience. Tracking did little to help students direct their studies. Indeed, humanistic psychologists would be quite uncomfortable with progressive reformers' narrow understanding of talents and with the way reformers used tests to direct students rather than letting students direct themselves.

To summarize, the rationales and the rhetoric used by those discussing the desirability of tracking emphasized utilitarian and rights-oriented priorities. The terms "democracy" and "human potential" were invoked but their meaning was shaped by more fundamental commitments to human capital development (vocational training), cognitive development, utility, and equality of opportunity.

THE RECENT DEBATE

Over the course of the past decade, both practitioners and the policy community have again debated the desirability of tracking and ability grouping. Most have opposed the practice. Researchers have argued that tracking "make[s] it difficult to achieve either excellence or equality" and that it "contributes to mediocre schooling for most secondary students" (Oakes, 1986a, 12). The Carnegie Council on Adolescent Development (1989) recommends that middle schools "ensure success for all students through elimination of tracking by achievement level" (9). And the National Governors' Association (1990) has "challenge[d] educators to eliminate ability grouping and tracking."[7]

Arguments used both to support and to criticize ability grouping today are strikingly similar to those advanced in the 1920s. The same technical matters are debated. Are teachers more effective in classrooms with students of relatively similar ability? Do heterogeneous class settings slow down academically talented students? Is the assignment of students to different ability groups or tracks based on merit?

Are students in low-track classes denied opportunities for future success?

As in earlier periods, utilitarian and rights-oriented logics and goals dominate these debates. More exactly, "arguments about the structured use of ability groups usually pit educational efficiency against social equity" (Schneider, 1989, 11). The concerns of humanists and democratic communitarians remain in the background. As before, plans to track students according to academic ability and vocational interests are compared with proposals to provide all students the same liberal education. Other possibilities, which will be discussed later in this chapter, receive no attention.

Oakes, in one of the most widely cited comprehensive studies of tracking practices in American schools, *Keeping Track: How Schools Structure Inequality* (1985), summarizes the most common argument against tracking. Her findings emphasize a rights-based concern for equality of opportunity and a utilitarian concern for maximizing aggregate achievement.

> Certainly students bring differences with them to school, but, by tracking, schools help to widen rather than narrow these difference. Students who are judged to be different from one another are separated into different classes and then provided knowledge, opportunities to learn, and classroom environments that are vastly different . . . schools seem to have locked themselves into a structure [tracking] that may unnecessarily buy the achievement of a few at the expense of the many. (Oakes, 1986a, 17)

Much in this rhetoric mirrors the earlier discussions of tracking outlined above. The utilitarian arguments, in fact, have barely changed. As before, analysts look at achievement data and debate whether tracking and ability grouping practices support or hinder student performance. Tracking's impact on equality and merit-based success also is still a matter of great concern to policy analysts. However, to a greater extent than in earlier periods, when differences in performance are noted, they are characterized as a problem to be minimized. Finally, individuals are still compared with others on the basis of narrowly defined academic criteria.

Utilitarian Concerns and Tracking

Studies of tracking's effects are numerous (see Slavin, 1990; Kulik and Kulik, 1982; and Rosenbaum, 1980, for reviews). As was common in earlier periods, those assessing the desirability of tracking and ability grouping implicitly equate achievement test scores with utility and ask, "Does ability grouping influence student achievement?" (Rosenbaum, 1980, 365).

Tracking's proponents write that such practices often are most efficient and that they permit all students, particularly talented students, to fully achieve academically. This perspective is commonly advanced by those who support gifted and talented education (see Feldhusen, 1989; Allan, 1991). Reviewers of the literature note that students in gifted programs learn more than similar students in nontracked classes or even within class groupings (Kulik and Kulik, 1982). Allan (1991) writes, for example, "Gifted and high-ability children show positive academic effects from some forms of homogeneous grouping. . . . The preponderance of evidence does not support the contention that [other] children are academically harmed by grouping" (65). One article went as far as to call gifted students "our most neglected natural resource" (Lyon, 1981).

Tracking's critics also focus on utilitarian concerns. Those who summarize studies of tracking's effects on achievement write that the "overall achievement effects were found to be essentially zero at all grade levels" (Slavin, 1990, 471). This, they believe, neutralizes utilitarian arguments for tracking. They then argue against tracking, writing that it has no meaningful effects on achievement and that it conflicts with commitments to equality (see Slavin, 1991; Oakes, 1986a).

Others, especially those writing for the popular press and the policy community, argue as John Peterson did in *The American School Board Journal* (1989) that "tracking students by their supposed ability levels can derail learning" (38). They write that tracking diminishes the achievement of low-ability students. Headlines from articles on tracking in popular magazines include "Is Your Child Being Tracked for Failure?" (*Better Homes and Gardens*), "The Label That Sticks" (*U.S. News and World Report*), and "Tracked to Fail" (*Psychology Today*) (in Allan, 1991, 62). These critics also write that our nation's economic prosperity demands that all students receive challenging academically oriented preparation and that tracking often lowers expectations.

> Schools must challenge all students to reach high standards. Yet ability grouping in the elementary grades and tracking in the secondary grades prevent this, especially for students placed in the lower groups. There, low expectations become self-fulfilling prophecies. (National Governors' Association, 1990, 17)

It is important to note here that analysts attend only to some forms of utility—those which are equated with economic progress and cognitive development. Analysts do not ask, for example, whether students find homogeneous grouping to be more enjoyable than heterogeneous grouping. The boredom, sense of inadequacy, or frustration students might experience in different settings is generally ignored by policy analysts except insofar as these feelings affect academic performance. Similarly, studies of vocational education programs assess their impact on students' employment rates and earnings. They do not systematically assess whether students who get to spend part of their school day learning to be beauticians or auto mechanics, find school to be more enjoyable or more meaningful than similar students who follow a liberal arts curriculum.

Rights Theory and Tracking

Although the focus of utilitarian concerns today closely parallels those raised in the first decades of this century, analysis concerned with equality, justice, and meritocracy has changed in important ways. Seventy-five years ago progressives argued that tracking enabled the delivery of equally appropriate educational services to individuals of varied academic abilities. Their opponents responded that equality of opportunity was threatened by the provision of separate curricula in high schools. Today, few emphasize the value of vocational training or other forms of curricular differentiation. The policy community has a far stronger commitment to providing all students with a liberal education. Indeed, both the nation's governors and the President currently support national standards that will promote "equitable educational opportunity for all Americans." These standards will apply

> to all students. . . . [And] poor initial performance should not be used to divert students into less demanding courses with lower expectations but rather must lead to improved instruction and redoubled effort. (National Council on Education Standards and Testing, 1992, 10)

Current rights-based critiques of tracking fault the system for "making inequality" (Rosenbaum, 1976) by providing high- and low-track students with vastly different "access to knowledge," "opportunities to learn," and "classroom climate." Tracking is charged with "exaggerat[ing] the initial differences among students rather than [providing] the means to better accommodate them" (Oakes, 1986a, 14). Qualitative investigations also have indicated that these placements reflect a student's race, class, and parental influence as well as test scores and teacher evaluations (Cicourel and Kitsuse, 1963; Oakes, Selvin, Karoly, and Guiton, 1992; Useem, 1990). In short, "the fairness of placement practices is questionable" (Oakes, 1992, 14).

Rights-oriented proponents of tracking counter by writing that most evidence indicating that tracking assignments reflect class and race rather than merit is based on the high correlation between race, class, and track assignment. Many quantitative studies that control for student motivation, student ability, and other relevant variables do not support these conclusions (see Rehberg and Rosenthal, 1978). In addition, writers argue that students frequently choose their tracks. As Rosenbaum (1980) states:

> Free choice is central to the justification of curriculum grouping. If individuals or their parents freely choose their curriculum, then questions about institutional discrimination do not arise. (377)

Finally, proponents of gifted education and parents who want their children placed in high-ability tracks can counter appeals for heterogeneous grouping by arguing that such plans threaten individual rights. Critics of tracking are asking high-ability students to give up their accelerated curriculum so that they can stimulate the others. "It is morally questionable," Susan Allan (1991) writes in her defense of ability grouping, "for adults to view any student's primary function as that of role model to others" (64). Walzer (1983) aligns this argument squarely with the logic of rights theorists. Those who want to abolish what Walzer calls "talent tracks," hope to distribute the most academically able students

> throughout the school so as to stimulate and reinforce the others. This looks like using the bright students as a resource for the less bright, treating the former as means rather than as ends. (Walzer, 1983, 220)

Walzer does not, however, support tracking.

Muddled Rhetoric

Where do these arguments take us? Despite calls for reform, tracking and ability grouping are still common. There are powerful groups on both sides of this issue. Researchers and other critics of tracking argue that tracking promotes neither equity nor excellence, but their arguments have yet to bring widespread change. The technical challenges associated with detracking, cultural commitments to the importance of student differences, and efforts by "high-ability" students and their parents to maintain their special status and extra resources have all constrained attempts to shift practice (Oakes, 1992).

Faced with these competing pressure groups, policy makers and practitioners are often less consistent than they might like to admit. Rosenbaum (1980) reminds us, for example, that "the Coleman report found that many school administrators denied that ability grouping existed in the same schools where a majority of teachers and students responded that it did exist" (362). This tension and the ambiguity it promotes are also evident in policy documents. A major report issued by the National Governors' Association (1990) takes a historic stand when it "challenge[s] educators to eliminate ability grouping and tracking." But it then continues:

> Eliminating these practices does not require ending special opportunities for students, such as gifted and talented or Advanced Placement courses. Nor does it mean abandoning special education or remedial programs for those who need additional services or assistance. (17)

Finally, educational researchers at eminent universities almost unanimously denounce tracking in high schools and then sit on admissions committees in which they try to accept only the "best" candidates.

These internal contradictions indicate that the consensus and political will needed to act decisively on tracking policy have yet to be achieved. They also clearly demonstrate that even when educators agree that equity and excellence are their primary concerns, many normative and technical issues can prevent consensus on policy. What is less clear, but no less important, is the way dominant utilitarian and rights-oriented concerns have structured discussions of tracking and led to voluminous and valuable debates, but have marginalized other important perspectives. Democratic communitarian and humanistic perspectives are rarely present in mainstream discussions of tracking policy.

HUMAN POTENTIAL AND TRACKING

The rhetoric that surrounds tracking discussions includes firm commitments to "realizing potential," "fully developing talents," and "tailoring programs to individual differences." The substance of these commitments, however, would disappoint humanistic psychologists, whose concerns rarely enter discussions of tracking.

This is surprising. Starting with the ancient Greeks, educational theorists have talked in a variety of ways about gearing educational experiences to align with human potential and desires. Clearly, tracks could be designed to permit students with differing interests to pursue different paths. Nonetheless, although critics and proponents of tracking often debate issues of research methodology, offer diametrically opposed interpretations of similar findings, and worry about different student groups, they think about human potential in the same way. They focus on measures of academic ability, on attainment of degrees and credentials, and on the development of human capital.

Two Examples

Slavin (1991), for example, invokes the rhetoric of psychological humanists when he writes:

> I do believe that schools must recognize individual differences and allow all students to reach their full potential, and they can do this . . . without turning to across-the-board between-class grouping. (69)

On the surface such a claim might seem satisfactory to humanists. But the context, an article that focuses on the impact of grouping strategies on tests of academic achievement, exposes the narrow nature of Slavin's goal. The "individual differences" he refers to are differences in academic abilities. "Reach their full potential" is the phrase he uses— a more accurate phrase would have been "get the highest scores possible on tests of academic skills and knowledge."

Similarly, the authors of *A Nation at Risk* write:

> Our goal must be to develop the talents of all to their fullest. Attaining that goal requires that we expect and assist all students to work to the limits of their capacities. (National Commission for Excellence in Education, 1983, 13)

The data presented in this report and the rationales provided for its policy proposals both reflect an academic orientation. The authors speak of the need to develop students' "talents" and "capacities," but quite specific meanings are ascribed to these terms. This landmark treatise on the imperative of school reform makes no mention of developing students' artistic or physical talents and pays no attention to students' emotional, creative, or interpersonal capacities. The focus is on competition in the world economy. Inadequate development of human capital has placed our "nation at risk."

In short, when policy analysts assess "the fulfillment of student potential," their indicators of potential (dropout rates and test scores) reveal that they mean something much more specific. What they really are concerned with is the fulfillment of students' potential to master academic subjects and to do well in both college and the workplace.

The Humanist Critique

Carl Rogers (1983) neatly summarizes humanists' concerns regarding the mainstream focus on academic abilities: "Such learning involves the mind only. . . . It does not involve feelings or personal meanings; it has no relevance for the whole person" (19). When policy makers and analysts speak of changes that will permit students to "fulfill their potential," they do not mean their potential to make long and lasting friendships, to become mediocre at hobbies they enjoy, or, more generally, to pursue the full range of experiences humanists associate with a meaningful and fulfilling life. In short, humanistic psychologists would object to analysis that equates "poor academic performance" with "poor human performance." They believe that the mainstream approach shows little respect for the diverse range of human interests, aptitudes, and needs. Moreover, by granting primacy to a narrow understanding of growth, educators may pass on to students values that discourage them from exploring their full range of capacities.

The significance of this critique for discussions of tracking policy becomes clearer when one recognizes the interdependence of "human potential" and "equality of opportunity" within mainstream discussions of tracking policy. As Oakes (1986b) explains in her "attempt to make explicit the prevailing conceptions of equality and schooling":

> Equal educational opportunity means equal opportunity to develop quite fixed individual potential (intelligence and abilities) to its limit through individualized effort in school, regardless of such irrelevant background characteristics as race, class, and gender. Providing equal opportunities to develop individual potential has instrumental value to both individuals and society. (61)

Oakes criticizes this definition, but she and other critics of tracking do not forcefully attack its narrow conception of either equal opportunity or human potential. Their focus remains on equal access to academic goals and human capital. They worry about stereotypes and lowered expectations. They criticize the ideology behind tracking for failing to see that "high status knowledge is equally appropriate for all" (Oakes,

1986b, 74). To ensure students equal development of human potential, they propose that all students receive a liberal education.

But does this attempt to provide all students "high status" knowledge conflate two separate concerns—quality and equality? A standardized curriculum may equalize educational experiences without improving them. If an academically oriented education is narrow and traditional, if it fails to meet the needs of the whole child and to develop students' full potential, then the answer provided by humanists would not be to offer this educational plan to everyone.

Those who believe that all students should receive a liberal education generally focus on English, history, science, math, and occasionally a foreign language. At times they hope that educators will cross disciplinary boundaries and integrate the teaching of literature and history, but this, for them, is a radical change. They fail to consider or in some cases reject the possibility that an education that emphasizes alternative priorities could still be first-rate.

Perhaps the strongest statement on this topic appears in the *Paideia Proposal*. Written by Mortimer Adler (1982), but the product of an esteemed committee that included Ernest Boyer, Alonzo Crim, and Theodore Sizer, this report stated forcefully:

> The one-track system of public schooling that *The Paideia Proposal* advocates has the same objectives for all without exception. . . . All side-tracks, specialized courses, or elective choices must be eliminated. Allowing them will always lead a certain number of students to voluntarily downgrade their own education. (15, 21)

This approach guards against the possibility that attempts to respond to student differences will lead to unequal and unjust treatment—a worthy concern. In the process, however, these policy advocates sacrifice an option with which few psychological humanists would part—the right to create a range of alternative educational programs.

In Defense of Tracking

Humanistic psychologists would criticize tracks that "offer" students less experienced teachers, lots of worksheets, low expectations, and exposure to disciplinary problems. Such arrangements limit students' future options and align poorly with their current interests and needs. At the same time, the alternative proposed by tracking's critics—a common academic curriculum—may serve some students well, but its uniformity has significant costs. As Nel Noddings (1992b) explains, the system requires that many students experience 12 years of frustration and possibly failure before they can pursue their interests and talents more directly:

> Children who are successful in [school] are prepared *by that very achievement* for further academic excellence and positions of leadership. But children who may someday be excellent tradespeople or artisans are "prepared" for those endeavors by failure in school. . . . Must our mechanically and artistically talented children suffer twelve or more years of failure or near-failure before they are to find [an alternative compatible with their interests or talents]? (5, emphasis in original)

Consequently, while a commitment to equality leads mainstream critics of tracking to recommend a common curriculum for all, it would probably lead those committed to humanistic goals to recommend improved tracking options, structures, and procedures. Rather than assuming that the academic priorities of some students should guide the education of all students, humanistic psychologists would likely support a system that permitted and encouraged much greater variation. They would want students, parents, and educators to have the flexibility to design programs that reflected academic and developmental needs as well as nonacademic interests.

A Possible Plan

What might this alternative system look like? This question has received relatively little attention from policy analysts who either criticize or promote tracking. It is also difficult to answer. In fact, although humanistic critiques of tracking discussions are relatively straightforward, humanist psychologists' positive program is far from certain.

Humanist psychologists would likely seek wholly new forms of tracking rather than simply modifications of traditional tracking arrangements. For example, tracks currently are designed for large groups of students. Often, however, student interests are relatively unique. Humanistic psychologists might want educators to have the flexibility to design tracks with independent studies and internships for individuals and for small groups of students with particular interests. Currently, most schools grant few students this flexibility, and these specialized programs are marginal additions to relatively full schedules. Humanists would likely argue that these tracks could constitute half or even more of a student's program.

In all likelihood, most specialized tracks would be designed for sizable groups of students rather than for individuals. Interests, rather than career goals or academic ability, would determine students' track selection. For instance, groups of students might focus on the arts, science and technology, child care and development, construction, or politics and public policy.

These tracks would differ from traditional structures in at least three important ways. First, track placement would not depend on academic ability, and the associated curriculum would not imply a choice between academic and vocational goals. Students in the science and technology group might spend time learning how to repair engines, experimenting in laboratories, and studying properties of chemical bonds. Students focusing on child care and development might work in a nursery, study child and adolescent psychology, and survey the need for child care in the community. Second, these tracks would vary from class to class depending on the particular interests of participants. Finally, unlike current tracking arrangements, which are relatively permanent, humanists would want students to experiment and change tracks as their interests shifted. These tracks would be numerous, flexible, and relatively fluid. Students along with educators would take part in their design.

Humanistic psychologists might be comfortable with the kind of plan outlined above. But they might say that many of the most complicated procedural questions have not been addressed. Which potential should schools strive to develop? How can students be helped to make choices that reflect their own values, rather than those conditioned by society? How can educators balance the need to respond to a student's particular interests and desires with the need to maintain further options? These three questions are discussed below.

1. *Which potential should schools strive to develop?* Mainstream analysts spend little energy considering varied understandings of human potential. They simply equate the pursuit of academic excellence with the realization of a student's potential. Psychological humanists, in contrast, expend significant energy helping students identify the nature of the goals they hope to pursue.

The question of direction is complex because one's potential is uncertain. An acorn, Israel Scheffler (1985, 42–43) points out, can become either an oak tree or food for a squirrel. Similarly, students have the potential to become many things. Is one alternative "better" than another? Humanistic educators want to help students make such decisions.

How would they help? Humanists believe that students will choose wisely if offered guidance and freed from the constraints of authority figures and cultural norms. Facilitators in humanistic class-rooms want to help direct both the form and the focus of students' educational experiences. They would not remain neutral when students made decisions regarding track selection.

As Adrian Underhill (1989) explains, humanistic educators often exercise "authoritative power" but not "authoritarian power." She writes that power is exercised appropriately if the interests of the student and not those of the teacher, the parent, or the nation guide teachers' efforts to direct students. These interests are understood to encompass the full range of priorities discussed in Chapter 4 and not the narrow goals emphasized in mainstream discussions. To further safeguard against the abuse of power, humanistic educators often give students opportunities for input. They may, for example, propose a direction and then say, "What do you think?" Or "What are the important issues for you?" (Underhill, 1989, 255).

Humanistic educators are not passive. Students' choices regarding track selection are influenced by the options teachers mention, those they advocate, and those they, in collaboration with students, are able to deliver. These educators use their influence to help students focus on and realize humanistic goals. They offer alternatives to the narrow vocational and academic goals mainstream analysts often put forward when assessing tracking.

This much said, many complexities associated with identifying appropriate educational directions or tracks remain. Two issues related to this task are discussed below.

2. *How can students be helped to make choices that reflect their own values, rather than those conditioned by society?* This question is far easier to state than it is to resolve. First, many philosophers and social critics would question the validity of the distinction it implies. They would argue that it is a mistake to think of students as possessing innate values that can be distinguished from those fostered by society. However, while these critics might be successful in undermining the theoretical coherence of the model put forward by humanistic psychologists, the salience of the humanists' concern remains. Few deny humanists' claim that social norms and pressures often misdirect students' expectations and goals. For example, humanists, like others, worry that a variety of social pressures often lead female students to systematically refrain from choosing to pursue or develop interests in mathematics, science, and technology. This concern is similar to that expressed by educators who worry that societal stereotypes often bias students' track assignments. If humanists and those in the mainstream point to a similar problem, however, they respond differently.

Mainstream analysts want track placement based on objective meritocratic criteria. As described in detail earlier, they expend considerable effort evaluating the extent to which such conditions hold. Humanists, in contrast, would not frame the issue in terms of fairness. *They would view the students' experience of choosing a track as an important part of the learning process.*

In ideal circumstances, decisions regarding track placement would be an important outcome of a counseling relationship between a student and his or her teacher. This relationship would demand trust, time, and shared respect. Students would be asked to consider their interests, past experiences, and future possibilities. "The notion is that something is there but is hidden, swamped, distorted [by exterior forces]" (Maslow, 1968a, 688). It is the therapist/teacher's role to help the student sort through these complexities. Humanists would recoil at the thought that such decisions should be made with reference to the kind of standardized or objective criteria mainstream analysts seek. Tracking decisions, they would argue, are personal and subjective decisions.

3. *How can educators balance the need to respond to a student's particular interests and desires with the need to maintain further options?* A common rationale for providing all students with a liberal education is that such an education permits future learning. As Adler (1982) writes in defense of this policy agenda, "Schooling, basic or advanced, that does not prepare the individual for further learning has failed" (11). Humanists would attack the programmatic implications that often result from this argument. They directly question analysis that equates preparation for college (a liberal education focusing on certain academic disciplines) with preparation for future growth opportunities. Those best prepared for college are sometimes the least prepared for life.

This critique, however, does not refute the need for balance. Humanists would agree with the mainstream contention that much of what learning and growth enables, is the ability to learn and grow more. Although often resisted initially, basic literacy skills, exposure to politics and poetry, instruction in a foreign language, and experience on a stage all have the potential to enlarge a student's capacity to consider alternatives and chart his or her own course. Humanists, along with mainstream analysts, worry that if students focus exclusively on special or immediate interests they may constrain future growth in two important ways. First, they will limit their exposure to many ideas and opportunities that they might find motivating. Second, their specialized focus may not develop certain affective qualities and cognitive skills that make possible other opportunities for further growth.

To guard against these possibilities, it seems likely that humanistic educators would want to balance provision of opportunities to explore particular interests with access to educational experiences that broaden students' awareness of alternative directions. Like mainstream analysts, they would debate the pedagogic and curricular implications of this concern. The terms of their discussion, however, would be somewhat different.

First, humanists would likely agree with mainstream analysts that disciplinary knowledge (e.g., science, history, math, English) broadens students' awareness of possibilities and provides skills needed for their pursuit. However, they would be far more challenging of many common beliefs about the importance of particular learning goals. Noddings (1992b) points out, for example, that it is common for mainstream educators to speak of the need for all students to learn mathematics. But where, she asks, is the evidence? Clearly, students need to be able to perform basic arithmetic. But do all need to know algebra and geometry? Do many jobs require such skills? Does the ability to determine the area of a triangle, when given its height and its base, foster growth? Is it a vitally important ability? Why?

Humanists would criticize mainstream discussions of "essential" educational experiences for focusing too much on academic knowledge and skills, and they would be frustrated by the lack of attention given to other aspects of development. Why, for example, is it generally considered essential to provide all students access to a course in biology, with labs that help them learn about mitosis and photosynthesis, but not important to give all students an opportunity to discuss and practice parenting skills in conjunction with an academically rigorous exploration of issues related to child development?

Mainstream discussions of core knowledge and essential experiences rarely include systematic attention to students' social and psychological needs. How, humanists might ask, can we ensure that all students have access to creative outlets, opportunities to develop their interpersonal abilities, and chances to partake in peak experiences? How can we ensure that students will have a therapeutically oriented component of their education? Inattention to these issues can constrain the range of human development. Humanists, like mainstream analysts, would recognize the importance of certain "core" educational experiences. The content of this core, however, would be different.

Humanistic Concerns and Mainstream Tracking Rhetoric

This educational agenda requires dramatic departures from traditional practice. As a result, those pursuing humanistic goals in mainstream policy environments face significant obstacles. Below I note three important differences between mainstream and humanistic orientations. I do this both to summarize humanistic perspectives on tracking and to underscore their lack of ideological alignment with mainstream analysts who talk about helping students "realize their full potential."

First, humanistic psychologists would want respect for social, emotional, and psychological growth to be central to the rhetoric of educational goals and to receive systematic consideration when analysts design and evaluate varied tracking proposals. These issues are raised by mainstream analysts who worry, for example, about tracking's effects on self-esteem. However, their interest in this topic is most commonly framed in terms of its effects on students' scholastic performance and not on their psychological growth as an end in its own right.

Second, humanists would reject the implicit acceptance of the occupational hierarchy that is commonplace in mainstream discussions of tracking. Humanists' respect for the full range of human capacities would lead them to reject assumptions embedded in mainstream discussions of tracking that favor abstract analytic ability over practical skills. They also would reject the notion that professions that require a college degree are more worthy than those that do not. This perspective contrasts sharply with the emphasis schools place on sorting students and, more generally, with an economic and social system driven largely by rewards based on these kinds of comparative judgments.

Finally, humanistic educators would reject mainstream beliefs regarding appropriate measures of talent, ability, and human capital. They would criticize the academically oriented standards put forward in both secondary and postsecondary schools. The constraint imposed by these standards is substantial. As long as institutions of higher learning and employers judge and reward individuals primarily by their attainment of academic skills and credentials, those who pursue what humanists regard as more well-rounded development will be sacrificing numerous opportunities.

DEMOCRATIC COMMUNITARIAN THOUGHT AND TRACKING POLICY

Democratic communitarians would criticize the content of tracking discussions more for what is absent than for what is discussed. They would be concerned with the impact of tracking and ability grouping on both achievement and equity. However, although the struggle for fair and effective schools is important, it differs in significant ways from the pursuit of democratic community.

Over the course of the past 10 years substantial attention has been given to the social implications of tracking. Analysts have studied students' attitudes about themselves, their peers, other cultures and races, and the formation of students' career expectations. Some researchers have also looked at students' social behavior. This follows "over 50 years of research [on] ability grouping [that was designed] almost exclusively to ascertain its achievement outcomes" (Rosenbaum, 1980, 363). Democratic communitarians would find much value in this new research direction.

First, mainstream analysts highlight the costs of within-school segregation by demonstrating the impact of track placements on students' perceptions of themselves and others. Slavin's (1987) discussion of "ability grouping and its alternatives," for example, begins with the words of a student.

> I felt good when I was with my (elementary) class, but when they went and separated us—that changed us. That changed our thinking, the way we thought about each other, and turned us into enemies toward each other—because they said I was dumb and they were smart. (32)[8]

When track placements are highly correlated with race or class, the social costs of these perceptions are magnified.

Mainstream research on the treatment of students in different tracks and on the permanence of track assignments also would be of great interest to democratic communitarians. They would be deeply troubled by the findings of Oakes (1985) and others who show that students in high-ability tracks get far more stimulating, orderly, and rewarding school experiences than those in low-ability tracks. Like mainstream analysts, they would object to low-track curricula that provide vocational and/or basic skills education but fail to provide students with the analytic skills or knowledge base they will need to participate fully in a community's decision-making process.

Thus, some research and rhetoric on tracking does highlight democratic communitarian concerns. One must be careful, however, not to overstate this point.

Communal Rather Than Individual Achievement

The emphasis educators place on individual achievement is so much the norm that it hardly seems like a choice. Analysts routinely assess educational programs by examining the scores individuals receive on tests of cognitive skills. They also examine whether individuals receive an equal opportunity to succeed on these tests. Such issues dominate research on tracking. These are not, however, the primary concerns of democratic communitarians.

Democratic communitarians pursue social harmony. They want individuals to work together as they identify and pursue meaningful priorities. Although they clearly are concerned with the knowledge and abilities individual students develop, democratic communitarians focus primarily on communal rather than individual achievement. They want students to achieve common goals by working together. They emphasize goals that are not aggregates of individual preferences, but that reflect the needs of the group. "Ideally," Eliot Wigginton (1986) writes in describing the decision process on his class projects, "they forget about the student personalities involved and make decisions together that are for the good of the project" (406–7).

Do tracking policies affect the pursuit of this alternative agenda? Do they alter a group's capacity for democratic deliberation? The current debates on tracking focus attention on individual students' opportunities and outcomes. Policy analysts do not ask whether tracking promotes or inhibits students' ability to pursue goals collectively or how it shapes their commitment to and understanding of democratic communities. To study such issues, researchers might ask whether tracking practices reflect or reinforce the emphasis educational institutions place on individual differences and on meeting individual rather than collective needs. They also might ask whether tracking serves to insulate students from their schoolmates' capacities, needs, and desires. More specifically, researchers might assess the impact that placing students in homogeneous classes has on the way the students view their own and others' academic difficulties. Do they regard these difficulties as concerns for professional educators or as something classmates should be expected to respond to through, for example, formal or informal peer and cross-age tutoring?

Why ask these questions? Democratic communitarians hope to promote settings in which individuals and groups reach across lines both to help and to learn from each other. They would be troubled by the evidence presented earlier that indicates that tracking practices are likely to increase the degree to which students see themselves members of subgroups: small communities defined by intelligence, ethnicity, race, gender, and class, which decrease students' allegience to and sense of equal membership in the broader school community.

Moreover, communitarians emphasize the impact of context on the way individuals define themselves and conceive of their goals. Thus, communitarians might worry that tracking defines individuals as different in consequential and frequently inaccurate ways (i.e., smart, dumb, college-able, failing, successful, average). Do these socially constructed identities extenuate our separateness at the same time that they lead individuals to accept as legitimate differential awards and opportunities? Or do tracking's critics overstate their case? Tracking may lead to some segregation, but students change tracks and have many opportunities to mix with a wide range of students throughout the school through participation in sports, art and drama groups, religious organizations.[9] Moreover, students may form friendships and cliques with others who share their race, class, academic orientation, and career goals, even if tracking is eliminated. Democratic communitarians would want researchers to assess the degree to which tracking reinforces rather than simply reflects these preexisting divisions within our culture.

Before concluding this section, an important exception is worth noting. Policy analysts who criticize tracking and advocate cooperative learning often praise cooperative rather than individualistic norms (Oakes, 1992; Slavin, 1987). Although examination of the research and rhetoric on this topic would demand its own essay, it is clear that these practices potentially offer much that democratic communitarians would value. Cooperative learning is desirable not simply because students "learn" more. Sharan's (1980) review of the literature on cooperative learning strategies demonstrates, for example, that these arrangements can promote "pupils' perceptions of mutual concern among peers" (248) and "positive interethnic contact under cooperative conditions" (258). This approach can be structured to model for students what democratic communitarians view as desirable forms of social interaction around meaningful issues.

It is also clear that some policy analysts who support cooperative learning do not focus on these goals. Many policy analysts' arguments for cooperative techniques are based primarily on claims that these techniques are effective means of promoting academic achievement. For democratic communitarians, in contrast, it matters what the students are working collectively to achieve. The way the goals are selected and the factors that motivate participants also matter. Furthermore, while it is true that many analysts today extol the values of cooperative rather than individualistic norms in schools, cooperative settings are not necessarily democratic. Workers in McDonald's cooperate. Indeed, teaching students to cooperate is often promoted as an economic imperative. The crucial question is whether a particular form of cooperative learning aligns with the ideals of democratic communities. Some forms of "group work" and "cooperative learning" may reinforce status hierarchies, bolster the traditional emphasis on abstract academic subject matter, further the traditional emphasis on academic subject matter, ignore consideration of societal needs, and rely on narrow forms of self-interest to motivate participants (Kohn, 1992; Sapon-Shevin and Schniedewind, 1992). Thus, neither heterogeneous grouping nor cooperative learning necessarily furthers democratic agendas. Democratic communitarians would push analysts to make careful distinctions regarding these issues.

Claims That Tracking Has an Adverse Impact on Democracy

At times, mainstream critics of tracking speak directly about democracy. They say that tracking threatens this goal in three ways. First, tracking's critics state that tracking is undemocratic because it promotes unequal opportunities. Second, they contend that detracking would strengthen our democracy by promoting greater cultural unity through the development of shared experiences and a shared vocabulary. Third, they write that tracking prevents adequate training for participation in the democratic process. By examining these claims I assess the differences between democratic communitarian and mainstream understandings of democracy and the impact of this difference on the analysis of tracking.

Unequal Opportunities. Mortimer Adler (1982) wrote that

> [a] democratic society must provide equal educational opportunity not only by giving to all its children the same quantity of public education—the same number of years in school—but also by making sure to give to all of them, all with no exceptions, the same quality of education. (4)

Is Adler correct? He claims that John Dewey would support his contention that to foster a democratic society we need "the same objectives for all without exception"(15). I believe that Dewey and other democratic communitarians would disagree with Adler. This is not to say that democratic communitarians reject the importance of equality of opportunity—they don't. But their understanding of equality is different.

Democratic communitarians would criticize this formulation of equality of opportunity because it has led analysts to focus on providing similar rather than similarly appropriate educational experiences. Oakes (1985), for example, criticized the movement toward tracking and comprehensive high schools for promising "something for everyone [but not] the same thing for everyone" (21). Using a parallel kind of argument, democratic communitarians would likely complain that mainstream commitments to fairness have resulted in commitments to sameness.

Democratic communitarians want equal respect for citizens, not equal treatment.[10] They believe students will make different kinds of contributions to society's growth. Consequently, democratic communitarians might emphasize the value of engaging students in collective enterprises where they would have the opportunity to contribute in different ways toward a common goal. Suppose, for example, that a heterogeneous class was asked to devise an ad campaign. A product would need to be selected, surveys designed and administered, commercials for television and radio developed, an advertising budget created, ethical issues considered, and so on. Students with differing academic, artistic, and social abilities could contribute in different, but equally valued, ways.

Such collective experiences may fill only a portion of a student's time in school. To ensure that all students are taught a set of essential skills,[11] are exposed to important information, and are able to explore personal interests, a variety of approaches may be used. Nonetheless, these collective undertakings are of central importance to democratic communitarians because they provide students with experiences that both build school communities and expose students to the nature and desirability of democratic and communal ties.

Democratic communitarians hope to foster democracy through pedagogy that fosters a social mode of learning, not by exposing all students to the same curriculum. Tracking structures, by bringing together students with shared interests, might make it easier to identify projects that class members find compelling. Students in a track that focuses on the media, for example, could easily work together on a newspaper. Similarly, students enrolled in a track that focuses on urban issues might investigate a city's policy on recycling by surveying community members, interviewing city officials, and researching the environmental concerns that sparked this effort.

To limit the segregatory potential of tracking systems, democratic communitarians, to a greater extent than humanistic psychologists, would consider carefully the desirability of different kinds of tracking plans. Systems that sorted students according to ability and/or particular vocational or college preparatory goals would be rejected. A track that focused solely on automotive repair, for example, might be unacceptable because it would likely reflect and reinforce gender and class divisions that exist within the broader community. In contrast, a track that focused on technology and included lab work in which all students learned about car engines might be supported.

Democratic communitarians would not equate democracy with equality of opportunity. In particular, they would be concerned that attempts to foster equality by removing tracks would lead to standardized educational experiences—experiences that did little to align students' education with their diverse needs, interests, and abilities. The risks that lead mainstream analysts to focus on standardization, however, would resonate with democratic communitarians. To the extent that they endorsed tracks, they would be careful to monitor the forms of association and status differentials that might result from particular tracking categories and to modify their plans when necessary.

Diminution of Cultural Unity. Mainstream critics of tracking write that with the growth of the comprehensive high school, educators abandoned their belief in the need for "common learnings to build a cohesive nation" (Oakes, 1985, 21). Would democratic communitarians share this concern? Will the abolition of different curricular tracks promote greater cultural unity and strengthen democracy through the development of a shared vocabulary? Is Hirsch (1987) correct when he writes that "[o]nly through a capacious and widely shared vocabulary [by which he means cultural literacy] can our democracy deal effectively with the contentious issues" of the "concrete politics, customs, technologies, and legends that define and determine our current attitudes and actions and our institutions" (103).

Richard Rorty (1989) essentially agrees. In a review of Hirsch's book, he writes that Deweyans like himself believe that high school students should be taught to see "themselves as heirs to a tradition of increasing liberty and rising hope. . . . As Hirsch quite rightly says, that narrative will not be intelligible unless a lot of information gets piled up in our children's heads" (22).

Others might agree that common curricular experiences can bring greater unity to increasingly diverse student populations, but not that this demands the kind of curricular goals Hirsch puts forward—nor, for that matter, the pedagogic approach Rorty implies. To be meaningful and democratic, this shared culture must be constructed through a continuous dialogue in which all can participate. If static information delivered by a teacher is simply "piled up in our children's heads," little progress will result.

Will common curricular experiences build a sense of shared commitments and understandings? Democratic communitarians would want this question subjected to systematic study. Currently, critics of tracking present no evidence that mixed-ability grouping or common curriculum offerings (similar science, math, English curriculum) lead students to develop a shared vocabulary that improves communication or creates a sense of unity that narrows group divisions. Making sure that all students read similar literature, study similar aspects of American history, dissect frogs, and learn to conjugate verbs in French or Spanish may not be a meaningful force for unity in a society divided by other, much more powerful factors (race, ethnicity, class, geography, social status). Educators may succeed in getting all students to study the same history lessons, but this may do nothing to diminish the social distance that separates cheerleaders from students in the band.

Such concerns may lead some democratic communitarians to criticize mainstream analysts who say they want group cohesion and improved communication on the grounds that the analysts focus too much on educational outcomes (exposure to particular subject matter) and too little on the educational process. Is the curriculum connected with students' experience? Do students explore this material collectively? Dewey and his followers would likely argue that democratic character, informed choice, and social unity are more readily pursued through pedagogy that has a meaningful social component than through a uniform or common curriculum that students experience as individuals.

Inadequate Training for Participation in the Political Process. Some opponents of tracking argue that it deprives students in lower tracks of the knowledge and skills needed to participate fully and effectively in a democratic society. Diane Ravitch (1985) writes of an

> ideal school [where] there would be no curricular tracking.... [All students] would gain the political and historical knowledge to participate effectively in the democratic process [and to] master the literacy that empowers people to read, write, think, and make judgments. (14–15)

Democratic communitarians might find this reason for rejecting tracking premature. Most would agree that low-track classes fail to provide students with the skills, knowledge, and critical perspectives needed to participate as equal members in debates on public policy. They also would applaud the efforts of educators to provide all students access to such opportunities. But they would not necessarily be

convinced that tracking systems inevitably fail to provide students
with the knowledge and analytic skills needed to participate in policy
discussions. One can imagine numerous tracking schemes in which all
tracks provide the analytic skills and knowledge necessary for meaningful citizenship. Rather than rejecting tracking outright, many democratic communitarians might argue that tracking proposals should
demonstrate their sensitivity to this issue. In other words, all tracks
should be structured so as to engage students in critical analysis of
significant social, moral, and political issues.

Democratic communitarian responses to these critics of tracking
might go one step farther. Some would question the assumption, common in mainstream discussions, that "a knowledgeable voter is a good
voter." Democratic communitarians believe that teaching students to
contribute as citizens requires the provision of much more than analytic skills. Just, humane, and responsive government springs as much
from individuals' value commitments and from the strength of interpersonal ties and ties to the community as from reasoned judgment.
Indeed, Jonathan Kozol ([1975] 1984) reminds us that "Gandhi, asked
once what it was that made him the most sad in life, is said to have
given this reply: 'the hardness of heart of the well-educated'" (180). By
focusing so fully on measures of cognitive growth, mainstream analysts interested in democracy may be missing much that matters. In
addition to providing students with knowledge and analytic skills,
democratic communitarians might want all tracks to include pedagogy
and curriculum that foster social sensitivity—an idea that will receive
detailed attention in Chapter 6.

Democratic Communitarians and Tracking Policy

In sum, many democratic communitarians would want to reorient discussions of tracking policy. They would find much mainstream research on tracking's effects helpful, but their focus and priorities would
be different. In particular, they would fear that the mainstream emphasis on cognitive goals and equality results in neglect of many concerns
that democratic communitarians value. For Dewey, "a democracy is
more than a form of government; it is primarily a mode of associated
living" ([1916] 1966, 87). To participate fully in democratic processes,
citizens need more than knowledge and analytic skills. Citizens must
learn how to identify and pursue common goals by letting the perspectives, priorities, needs, and abilities of community members inform
their behavior. Educators can further this goal by developing educa-

tional experiences that model these kinds of democratic relations and processes.

The neglect of these social goals is reflected in the options mainstream analysts consider and in their understanding of democracy. Critics of tracking argue that the practice should be eliminated—not reformed. Alternative tracking arrangements are barely discussed. Policy analysts' focus on equal access to college preparation pushes other concerns into the background. Similarly, although rhetoric connecting democracy and tracking exists, discussions of what is meant by democracy are rare. On most occasions when the term is invoked, it is considered for only one or two sentences. Slavin (1990) writes, for example, "Arguments in favor of grouping focus on effectiveness. . . . In contrast, arguments opposed to grouping focus at least as much on equity as on effectiveness and on democratic values as much as on outcomes" (474). The nature of these "democratic values" and their relevance is never discussed—it is handled as though it were self-evident. In addition, even those who write in more detail about democracy and tracking, such as Adler (1982), Oakes (1986a, 1992), and Ravitch (1985), devote little or no attention to the social orientation and classroom dynamics democratic communitarians want to develop. They reduce citizenship to voting and emphasize the need to provide all students with equal access to academic knowledge and analytic skills.

Were they to focus on developing this social orientation and to lessen their commitment to traditional discipline-based education, the possible value of alternative tracking procedures would likely become a subject of discussion. The tracking approaches advanced would differ from those currently in use. Tracks would reflect students' interests in topics, not students' place in a social, academic, or economic hierarchy. These tracks would afford students equal respect but not assume that this demands identical treatment. Moreover, the shared interests of students participating in these tracks would be used to promote collective educational activities that reflected and benefited from students' different priorities and talents.

PRIORITIES IN DEBATES ABOUT TRACKING

Rhetoric implying commitments to utility, equity, democracy, and human potential is common in discussions of tracking policy. Concern for utility and equality, however, dominate the substance of mainstream work on this issue.

Democratic communitarians would find much of the research on the segregatory impact of tracking responsive to their concerns. They also would be interested in the research demonstrating the unequal and poor-quality instruction students in low tracks receive. They probably would be less impressed with the generally superficial mainstream discussions that connect tracking to democracy. Their greatest frustration would likely be with the emphasis on individual (as opposed to collective) accomplishments that frames mainstream efforts to consider tracking's desirability. Finally, they might agree that promoting desegregation and more meritocratic arrangements by detracking is a step toward democratic community, but they would reject mainstream claims that imply that achieving such goals brings us close to the end of the journey.

Humanistic psychologists would be less charitable. They would disagree with most mainstream rhetoric and would pursue wholly different directions when considering tracking options. Particularly troubling for them would be the mainstream emphasis on the desirability of sameness. In addition, although they might agree that a liberal education can keep many options open, they would be highly critical of mainstream rhetoric that shows little respect for students who pursue nonacademic priorities. This rhetoric reinforces the notion that cognitive goals should be teachers' priorities.

Democratic communitarian and humanistic responses to research, analysis, and rhetoric on tracking policy would express many of the same themes. Both groups would emphasize the need to consider alternative conceptions of tracking, criticize efforts to provide all students the same curricula, stress the importance of creating curricula that respond to students' interests, and share mainstream concerns regarding the hierarchical and often unequal aspects of current tracking arrangements. Both groups would complain that mainstream analysts, in their effort to promote equality by abolishing tracks, neglect desirable alternatives.

6
School Choice

Choice is a Panacea.
—John Chubb and Terry Moe

In one of the most important educational documents of the 1990s, the authors of *America 2000* used the word "schools" often but the word "public" sparingly. It appeared just seven times in the 35-page document. Ironically, these seven references to public schools occurred only at those times when the document called their existence into question—during discussions of the school choice proposal set forth in the document. The proposal argued for broadening the definition of public schools to "include all schools that serve the public and are accountable to public authority, regardless of who [public, private, or religious groups] runs them" (Department of Education, 1991, 14). This proposal would have let public funds go to private and parochial schools—a policy that currently has many supporters.

Indeed, all presidents since Ronald Reagan have endorsed school choice proposals; support for this kind of reform began growing in the mid-1980s and as of early 1996 is still strong. When advocates state that school choice is a "national necessity" or a "prime means of improving the schools," their sentiments echoed by many governors, urban leaders, academics, and religious educators, democrats and republicans alike. By the end of 1993, school choice legislation had been introduced or was pending in 34 states, and 33 governors supported school choice in one form or another (Tucker and Lauber, 1994, 4).

This is not to say that consensus has been reached. Although many union leaders, religious groups, politicians, and business groups support school choice, the versions they back have significant differences. In addition, while proponents of school choice are numerous, many citizens, educators, and children's advocates remain skeptical. Given the magnitude of change that choice proposals imply, and the contentious and voluminous discussions such agendas have generated, it makes sense to consider the social, political, and ethical priorities that shape this debate.

What exactly is meant by school choice? What creates these impassioned dialogues? The proposals that fuel this controversy would give parents tuition vouchers or in other ways "free" parents to select the schools to which they send their children. Choice advocates hope to empower consumers by forcing schools to compete in a more or less free market. They hope that this system will "give parents and their children the leverage of competition to force change in the ossified . . . public schools" (*Wall Street Journal*, 1990, A12). Opponents see choice initiatives as "aggressively hostile to public schools" (*Los Angeles Times*, 1992, B5), as a retreat from the public commitment to educating all children, and as the "wrong surgery for sick schools" (*New York Times*, 1990b, A16).

Despite their differences, and the passion these differences provoke, it is striking that both sides agree on the general terms of the debate. Discussions and analysis of particular choice plans emphasize the importance of human capital development and focus on equity, efficiency, and excellence. These dialogues are valuable, but the dominance of mainstream priorities crowds out other important perspectives. Rather than assessing the strength of mainstream arguments, I demonstrate their commitment to human capital, utility, and justice. Then, in an effort to consider neglected alternatives, I suggest ways in which communitarian and humanistically oriented policy analysts might respond to mainstream calls for and against school choice.

GROWING ADVOCACY FOR SCHOOL CHOICE IN THE 1980S AND 1990S

Beginning around the mid-1980s, calls for school choice burgeoned:

> We propose an idea in the great American tradition: that you can increase excellence by increasing choice. (National Governors' Association, 1986, 67).

> For most goods and services—even vital ones such as food and shelter—the world has decided that markets are unambiguously better than politics. The ongoing transformation of Eastern Europe reaffirms this decision. (Chubb and Moe, 1991, 161)

> Our Goals 2000 proposal will empower individual school districts to experiment with ideas like chartering their schools to be run by private corporations or having more public school choice, to do whenever they wish to do as long as we measure every school by one high

standard: Are our children learning what they need to know to compete and win in the global economy? (Clinton, 1994, A9)

Why choice? Why choice now? The notion of funding private
schools with public money is not new. Neither are calls for school
choice within the public sector. What is new, and what recent proponents of school choice have built on, are widespread beliefs that our
educational system is failing, that this failure puts our "nation at risk,"
that public sector school reform initiatives probably will not make
schools more effective, and that competitive free markets will. The
compatibility of school choice proposals with the current policy climate does not guarantee their acceptance, but it has earned them serious consideration.

THE FREE MARKET RATIONALE FOR SCHOOL CHOICE: ALIGNMENT OF UTILITARIAN AND RIGHTS CONCERNS

One might expect choice proponents to talk exclusively in the language
of rights. The term "choice," after all, implies a form of freedom. Similarly, vouchers can be seen as a technical arrangement that frees individuals to pursue their own conception of the good. It is therefore not
surprising that Ron Brandt (1990/91a), the executive editor of the journal *Educational Leadership*, says in his overview of an issue devoted to
choice, "I find choice attractive because I like to see people doing what
they want rather than what they are required to do." On the same page
he continues, "Although I know something about the effectiveness of
various educational approaches, I wouldn't presume to say which are
best for every student" (3).

Given this clear rights orientation, it is surprising that utilitarian
sentiments informed the title of his commentary, "Conditions That Promote Excellence." Is choice a means to efficiency and utility or an end
in its own right? It is both.

A cozy combination of utilitarian and rights goals is used by many
who back school choice. This dual emphasis is possible because advocates endorse a particular kind of freedom—free markets. In perfectly
competitive free market systems, as individuals pursue their own conception of the good, they maximize aggregate utility. Choice proponents argue that their models simultaneously free individuals and improve educational services.

To provide a fuller appreciation of this perspective, I examine the
goals and logic of three prominent choice advocates. Specifically, I as-

sess the work of Milton Friedman and the more recent investigation by John Chubb and Terry Moe. Then, since these analysts advocate private school choice, I briefly consider the arguments made on behalf of public school choice.

The Libertarian Argument of Milton Friedman

Milton Friedman (1955) developed the modern economic rationale for a voucher or school choice system. He argued that providing parents with vouchers that could be used to purchase educational services at either public or independent schools would further both utilitarian and rights-oriented goals. His libertarian orientation is reflected in the fact that he sees vouchers as only a step in the right direction. In fact, Milton and Rose Friedman write in *Free to Choose* (1979) that they would, if possible, dramatically limit public financing for schools (except perhaps for "hardship cases") and eliminate compulsory attendance laws (151–52).

They "regard the voucher plan as a partial solution" (1979, 151). It improves on current arrangements in which only relatively well-off individuals can freely choose:

> [We can] send our children to private schools . . . [or] choose where to
> live on the basis of the quality of the public school system. (1979, 147)

Less well-off individuals have fewer options. Poor parents must accept their neighborhood schools regardless of their quality and emphasis. They cannot shop around for schools that satisfy their particular preferences.

Although freedom is their ultimate goal, Friedman and Friedman state that choice also might promote equity. They point out that few goods or services are distributed as unequally as public schooling. To make their point, they ask, "Are the supermarkets available to different economic groups anything like so divergent in quality as the schools?" (1979, 158). They argue that a free market would help to equalize the quality of service all students receive:

> The tragedy, and irony, is that a system dedicated to enabling all chil-
> dren to acquire a common language and the values of U.S. citizen-
> ship, to giving all children equal educational opportunity, should in
> practice exacerbate the stratification of society and provide highly un-
> equal educational opportunity. (1979, 148)

Friedman and Friedman also employ utilitarian logic and prize utilitarian goals. A choice system, they argue, will create competitive market situations in which producers (educators and the state) will respond to consumers' (parents' and students') needs and desires. Schools that do not respond to consumer demand will close, and new schools will open that will be better aligned with parent and student values. Friedman and Friedman describe numerous schools of choice that provide poor students a high-quality education for less money than public schools. In theory, then, choice initiatives can promote efficiency and effectiveness as well as equity and freedom.

The Efficacy Argument of Chubb and Moe

Although proposals for school choice and vouchers are not new, as confidence in public sector reform has declined, interest in school choice has grown dramatically. Numerous communities and several states and cities have recently implemented choice systems. John Chubb and Terry Moe's book *Politics, Markets, and America's Schools* provides the intellectual, rhetorical, and empirical support for many of these efforts.

Chubb and Moe's analysis is significantly different from that put forward by earlier choice advocates. Most earlier arguments for choice defined the policy problem in terms of liberty. Friedman and Friedman (1979; Friedman, 1955; also see Coons and Sugarman, 1978) stressed the importance of freeing parents to guide their children's education. In contrast, Chubb and Moe (1990) base their arguments on a utilitarian commitment to effectiveness. As they write, "This is a book about the causal foundations of effective schools" (185).

Their model builds on both organizational theory and a literature known as "effective schools research." They present empirical evidence that aims to demonstrate that schools of choice promote higher student outcomes and foster desirable forms of school organization and culture. More specifically, they find that particular school qualities such as clear goals, ambitious academic programs, strong leadership, and teacher professionalism lead students to achieve academically. In addition, they find that these qualities more commonly occur in schools that are subject to fewer bureaucratic regulations.

They then use High School and Beyond data[1] and organizational theory to argue that the form of governance influences the degree of regulation. Public schools are governed by systems of direct democratic control. In these systems, elected school boards select superintendents who exert centralized control over a district's schools. This method of governance fosters bureaucratic requirements that constrain effective leaders and prevent the development of flexible and truly professional school cultures. Thus, "the specific kinds of democratic institutions by which American public education has been governed for the last half century appear to be incompatible with effective schooling" (Chubb and Moe, 1990, 2). In contrast, schools that parents and students choose tend to have both fewer regulations and the organizational features that promote high achievement. In short, Chubb and Moe emphasize utilitarian concerns and argue from a theoretical and empirical base that our inadequate schools are the result of governance by direct democratic control.

Although primarily employing a utilitarian emphasis on test scores and efficiency, the authors are not completely inattentive to equity issues and other rights concerns. They want wealthy districts to contribute more money than poorer districts. They also recommend that state and federal support for the education of poor, handicapped, or otherwise disadvantaged students be distributed in the form of add-ons to the vouchers all students receive. This will provide an incentive for schools to admit them (220). They also "think it is unwise to allow [parents] to supplement their scholarship amounts with personal funds [since] such 'add-ons' threaten to produce too many disparities and inequalities within the public system" (220). They would, however, permit districts to spend different amounts of money on vouchers. As a result, students from poor or low-tax districts might not have large enough vouchers to attend schools in better funded districts.

Chubb and Moe's commitment to equality is markedly different from their interest in efficiency and excellence. Although theory and data drive their discussion of the institutional structures that promote effective schools, neither theory nor data are used to support their argument regarding the impact of their proposal on educational equity. The topic is considered in a few paragraphs on pages 220 and 221 of their book. Otherwise it is basically ignored. Their index provides 39 references to effective school organization and research. The words *equality, freedom,* and *liberty* do not appear in the book's index. Similarly, no references in the index are made to disadvantaged, at-risk, poor, or minority students.[2] In short, their pursuit of educational excellence is systematic; their discussion of educational equity and social justice is not.

The Argument for Public School Choice

Many choice advocates believe market arrangements will improve schools but fear that funding private schools with public money will erode citizens' commitment to public education and lead to greater inequality. They believe public school choice can provide needed safeguards while promoting meaningful change (see Raywid, 1985, for a review; also see Association for Supervision and Curriculum Development [ASCD], 1990). More specifically, public school choice plans are seen as a way to foster innovation, provide parents and students with a range of desirable options, promote desegregation, attract and retain committed educators, and use market forces to identify both successful and inadequate schools. Under this system, independent and religious schools cannot receive public money. "By using choice judiciously," Deborah Meier (1991) writes, "we can have the virtues of the marketplace without some of its vices, and we can have the virtues of the best private schools without undermining public education" (271).

Until recently, discussions of public school choice tended to focus on magnet schools. Magnet schools generally are designed by districts in an effort to provide high-quality specialized programs for students with particular interests or abilities. These programs also are frequently used to promote desegregation (Metz, 1990). Recently, proponents of public school choice have focused on creating charter schools. These schools are designed by teachers, students, parents, businesspeople, or other interested individuals. They receive their charter from the state or district, but then operate as relatively autonomous entities. As a result, this approach is seen by proponents as promoting the benefits of free market dynamics more effectively than did magnet schools. Many states currently are considering charter school legislation and nine states have begun implementing experimental charter programs (Tucker and Lauber, 1994).

LIBERAL CRITICS OF SCHOOL CHOICE PROPOSALS

If Chubb, Moe, and other choice advocates emphasize excellence and are less attentive to the possible impact of their proposal on equity, critics of school choice do the opposite. They charge that choice proposals jeopardize the ability of public schooling to promote equal outcomes and equality of opportunity. Just as market structures permit students to avoid troubled schools, they fear that those running schools of choice will structure admissions processes so as to avoid troubled students. They point to studies that indicate that public school choice, as currently practiced, sends funds to schools that serve only the most academically talented, the whitest, the best behaved, or the richest students. Other, less "desirable" students often are left without desirable options (see Moore and Davenport, 1990). As the editors of the *New York Times* ask, "What of the children left behind?" (*New York Times*, 1991b, A14).[3]

Those arguing in a manner more consistent with utilitarian concerns directly challenge Chubb and Moe's claim that a choice system will promote more effective schools. More specifically, critics (for example, Glass and Matthews, 1991; Rosenberg, 1990/91; Tweedie, 1990) question their research methods, the way they interpret their data, and the policy implications they derive from their analysis. Some point out that Chubb and Moe do not control for the fact that parents currently choosing to pay for their children's education probably place more emphasis on education than otherwise similar parents who use a neighborhood school. Others argue that the changes in achievement attributed to choice are small even if one accepts this methodological approach. Glass and Matthews (1991) write, for example, that even if one accepted Chubb and Moe's model, students attending a school that moved from the 5th percentile to the 95th percentile on their measure of autonomy would be expected only "to climb a month or so in grade equivalent units on a standardized achievement test" (26).[4]

These critics question the degree to which either public or private school choice will foster more effective schools. They do not, however, argue that choice will make schools less effective. Choice proposals rarely are rejected on utilitarian grounds. As the authors of *Public Schools of Choice* state, "The choice approach must ultimately earn its way or fail depending on how it responds to that concern [i.e., equity]" (ASCD, 1990, 28).

Much more could be said about these debates. My purpose, however, is to highlight the form of these arguments and not to assess the strength of particular claims. My point is that discussions by mainstream analysts regarding choice have been conducted almost exclusively within utilitarian and rights frameworks. When analyzing choice proposals, both critics and choice advocates focus on the same three goals: equity, efficiency, and excellence.

These concerns and the debates they spark are important. The impact of school choice on equity, efficiency, and excellence may be significant, and empirical evidence is scarce. Equally scarce, however, is consideration of alternative priorities. While the impact of various school choice initiatives on utility and rights deserves attention, the possible effect should be viewed from other vantage points as well. What is a likely impact of school choice on the formation of democratic communities? Will school choice initiatives lead educators to develop more schools that are attentive to humanistic concerns? How might policy dialogues change if these alternative perspectives helped to shape policy analysis? What data would be gathered by democratic communitarians and humanists, and how would they be assessed? What new policy directions might emerge? These two alternative perspectives are considered below.

COMMUNITARIAN COMMITMENTS AND CHOICE

During discussions of school choice policy, many issues that matter to democratic communitarians fail to receive systematic attention. Other issues are ignored completely. To gain a sense of these gaps, I map school choice policy discussions into the communitarian framework developed in Chapter 3. I begin by looking briefly at the alignment of school choice rationales with traditional communitarian commitments. I then consider how democratic communitarians might assess the impact of various choice plans on school governance procedures and student experiences.

The Communitarian-Choice Interface

In the past, choice proponents endorsed traditional communitarian commitments. Although Milton Friedman provided the modern economic rationale for choice, he was hardly the first to broach the subject in a policy arena. Catholics and other religious groups began arguing as early as in the 1840s that the government should subsidize parochial schools (see Perko, 1988; Tyack, 1974). Public school advocates fought these efforts. The debates that resulted were dramatically different from their modern counterparts. Liberal notions of equity, efficiency, and individual liberty were not central to the earlier discussions.

Religious educators hoped to maintain traditional communities. They did not want to create a market in which schools competed to satisfy consumers. Moreover, these schools were the product of a collective commitment to a cultural or religious perspective, not the result of choices made by autonomous individuals seeking to maximize satisfaction (Kraushaar, 1972; Carper and Hunt, 1984).

Catholics, for example, built a system of parochial schools to maintain their traditions and to insulate themselves from the Protestant bias prevalent in public schools. They wanted to provide their children with a religious education. They did not argue that parochial schools would teach academic skills more effectively. Similarly, the mainstream educators who rejected the notion of publicly funding religious schools did not emphasize efficiency, equity, or individual liberty. Instead, they championed the need for common schools. This interpretation, however, must be qualified. As Tyack and Hansot (1982) point out, the commitment of Protestant educators to common schools reflected both their desire to unify a diverse population and their often unquestioned belief that the schools should develop a "shared culture" that reflected the tenets of Protestant ideology.

In short, nineteenth-century battles over the desirability of school choice did not focus on equity, excellence, or efficiency. Participants fought for educational institutions that reflected their cultural and religious commitments.

Given the traditional communitarian orientation of earlier choice proponents, it is tempting to emphasize their differences from modern proponents, who prize competition. One might argue that early choice proponents were driven largely by commitments to particular religions, while current advocates hold near-"religious" commitments to free market ideology. It is important to note, therefore, the degree to which traditional communitarian concerns still motivate many supporters of choice, even though their rhetoric implies liberal commitments to freedom. For example, the rhetoric of President Reagan and President Bush may have stressed issues related to cognitive achievement, but their support for choice also reflected their commitment to religious constituents.

Democratic Communitarian Responses to Choice Proposals

Does school choice threaten democracy? Although the term "democracy" appears frequently in discussions of school choice, the connections between choice and democracy rarely are given systematic attention by policy analysts. Fortunately, some extensive analyses that highlight these issues recently have been completed (see Carnegie Foundation for the Advancement of Teaching, 1992; Wells, 1993; Henig, 1994). Generally speaking, however, critics do not respond to Chubb and Moe's (1990) assertion that

> [t]here is nothing in the concept of democracy to require that schools be subject to direct control by school boards, superintendents, central offices, departments of education, and other arms of government. (229)

Why, proponents of choice ask, must publicly funded schools be governed by school boards? Why can't citizens ask their legislators to design a different institutional arrangement? The terms of this arrangement would be products of a democratic process. In fact, choice advocates continue, those committed to democracy should support school choice since it frees individuals and since opinion polls consistently find that the public supports increasing school choice (see Finn, 1990).

Suppose that democratic communitarians assessed the desirability of school choice and responded to these calls for change—what might they say? Although policy analysts rarely adopt this perspective, work by Dewey and some contemporary political theorists can be used to structure an answer.

To highlight the ways in which democratic communitarian concerns would reorient discussion of school choice proposals, I consider how they might respond to the two major claims made by choice advocates. Specifically, I look at the claim that governance by direct democratic control should be eliminated and the assertion that this change would improve students' educational experiences.

Choice as a System of Governance—Reactions of Democratic Communitarians. The authors of *Politics, Markets, and America's Schools* write that our nation's educational shortcomings can be traced to our method of school governance. School boards and superintendents work in contentious political environments. Advocacy groups, professional organizations, teachers' unions, business leaders, and others constantly try to influence school policy. As these groups work to ensure that their "values get implemented [they] engineer the schools' behavior through formal constraints—[they] bureaucratize" (Chubb and Moe, 1990, 41). The resulting regulations deny school personnel the flexibility and professional school culture needed to operate effectively in contextually complex environments. As a result, student achievement suffers. In response to this problem, Chubb and Moe argue for "fundamental change"—for rejecting the current governance system of democratic control and for endorsing markets.

Democratic communitarians would define the problem differently. Like choice proponents, they would be troubled by the interest group politics Chubb and Moe describe. However, the inability of participants to work together toward a shared understanding of quality education would concern democratic communitarians much more than the impact of political battles on student achievement. For them, the dominance of interest group politics signals the need for a more fundamental change than the "fundamental change" choice advocates suggest.

Proponents of free markets hope to create an organizational structure in which individuals' self-serving behavior can be used to foster better schools. The problem facing democratic communitarians is different. It involves modifying this self-serving orientation. Democratic communitarians hope to develop forums in which educators, community members, parents, and students can struggle toward a shared set of goals for their children, and, more generally, their community. As Tyack and Hansot (1981) explain:

> Decision-making in education can provide a forum for discussing the kind of future we want as a society, not just as individuals. Such arenas for public discourse and action are hard to find. . . . [Discussions regarding public schools] generate valuable debates over matters of immediate concern, and offer a potential for community of purpose that is unparalleled in our society. (22–23)

For democratic communitarians, then, fostering a desirable governance process would be a major priority.

Communitarians also argue that choice advocates ignore the way that governance through markets threatens democratic communities. Members of democratic communities, they point out, take part in collective efforts toward common goals, and governance arrangements that utilize market forces subvert this process in two important ways: First, they encourage individuals to advance private interests. Second, they insulate a community's subgroups from interaction with those who hold alternative perspectives.

Amy Gutmann[5] (1987) directly addresses these issues when she asks, "Should parents or democratic communities be the primary authorities to choose among the legitimate purposes and methods of primary education?" (65). She concludes that voucher plans are undesirable because they fail to satisfy our collective interest in fostering democracy through education. She argues that the policies through which schooling can further this collective interest must be determined by debates among members of the community. "The problem with voucher plans is not that they leave too much room for parental choice but that they leave too little room for democratic deliberation" (70).

Michael Walzer (1983) places similar emphasis on the need for public deliberation. He states that the inability of parents and entrepreneurs to guarantee all children a quality education makes universal choice plans unacceptable:

> For the community has an interest in the education of children, and so do the children, which neither parents nor entrepreneurs adequately represent. But that interest must be publicly debated and

given public form. That is the work of democratic assemblies, parties, movements, clubs, and so on. (219)

The primary emphasis here is on the importance of democratic deliberation within a community. Democratic communitarians emphasize the need for inclusive forums and public debate. Although choice systems might be democratic in that they permit individuals to vote with their feet and are products of elected officials, these critics fear that school choice policies will inhibit the growth and maintenance of democratic communities. They will permit relatively well-off individuals to ignore the needs and concerns of fellow community members. Where systems of direct democratic control provide forums for citizens to discuss matters of great public concern while forging communal ties, choice systems encourage individuals to attend to private interests.[6]

Some policy analysts do criticize choice advocates for "rejecting the role of public deliberations concerning the purposes of education and denying the character of education as a public good" (Tweedie, 1990, 550). Often, however, when these concerns are raised, they are dealt with in less then one paragraph (see, for example, Cookson, 1991; Tweedie, 1990). Moreover, those who criticize the impact of choice on these alternative grounds lack a positive program. They say they worry that choice threatens democratic communities but, other than identifying their concern, they do not provide systematic evidence that the current system is democratic or provide proposals that aim directly at these issues.[7]

Both analysis and policy proposals are needed. Democratic participatory governance systems (school boards) can foster community but they commonly degenerate into battles between particular interest groups (Kirst, 1984). If policy analysts want to create governance practices consistent with democratic communitarian values, they will have to reform the system and engage numerous policy issues.

How local, for example, should school boards be? Would smaller districts help? Recent reforms in Chicago have created elected boards at every school. These boards set many regulations, hire their principal, control large parts of the budget, and can help determine the curriculum. Does this kind of grass-roots democracy create the kind of forums democratic communitarians desire? A related set of questions also seem pertinent. How can meaningful participation of parents who feel alienated from schools be fostered in large and diverse settings? When conflict surfaces, how can meetings be run so as to respect strongly held minority viewpoints while moving toward a common agenda?

The place of professional judgment within democratically controlled schools also must be examined. In what ways can important aspects of professional autonomy be protected? How should the policy-making roles played by teachers, administrators, parents, and school boards change when the focus of discussions shifts from pedagogy, to school finance, to graduation requirements, or to other topics? Can deliberation among school site personnel be made more consistent with democratic communitarian principles? What role might students assume in the governing process?

Questions such as these call out for debate, analysis, and creative solutions. Currently, however, they are marginal to most mainstream reform discussions. Educational reformers rarely even discuss school boards. Both the literature by academics on school reform and major policy statements such as *A Nation at Risk* and *America 2000* pay little or no attention to school boards. To the extent that research and policy analysis concerning school boards is done, it focuses on helping school boards "bring about better support and outcomes for students" (Danzberger, Kirst, and Usdan, 1992, xi). Analysts rarely ask how to create a process that generates what Tyack and Hansot (1981) refer to as "a community of purpose" (23). Reformers ignore John Gardner's challenge. They do not ask how boards that must represent diverse populations, can shift dynamics from the protection of narrowly defined interests to the formation of coalitions around common goals.[8]

Student Experience and School Choice—Reactions of Democratic Communitarians. Analysts who adopt democratic communitarian perspectives would not confine their attention to the governance process. Like mainstream analysts, they also would consider the probable impact of school choice on students' educational experiences. The form and focus of these considerations, however, would differ from those offered in the mainstream. As noted earlier, mainstream analysts ask questions like, "Will school choice increase the cognitive gains of participating students?" "Will it free parents and students to select schools that align with their own conception of quality education?" "Will it deny some students access to equal educational opportunities?" Democratic communitarians would certainly care about these concerns. Student achievement, parent and student satisfaction, and equality of opportunity are all important to democratic communitarians. Their main distinction from mainstream analysts would be reflected in the emphasis they placed on the following question: "Will systems of school choice promote democratic school communities?"

As Dewey pointed out, one can assess the degree of democracy within a community by considering two questions: "How numerous and varied are the interests which are consciously shared?" and "How full and free is the interplay with other forms of association?" (Dewey, [1916] 1966, 83). In line with these concerns, educational policy analysts might ask:

1. Will a given school choice proposal constrain or promote interaction among students of varied communities?
2. Will a given school choice proposal increase or decrease the number of interests students consciously share?

By considering these questions, we can explore how commitments to democratic communitarian values might broaden policy dialogues on school choice.

   1. *Will a given school choice proposal constrain or promote interaction among students of varied communities?* As noted above, some who support school choice do so in an attempt to use public monies to fund educational programs that emphasize a particular (often religious) vision of the good. This educational agenda impedes the formation and maintenance of democratic communities. Class-segregated, religiously oriented, or racially homogeneous school communities often come at the expense of a broader sense of democratic community. As Dewey writes:

> Wherever one group has interests "of its own" which shut it out from full interaction with other groups, . . . its prevailing purpose is the protection of what it has got, instead of reorganization and progress through wider relationships. (Dewey, [1916] 1966, 86)

Expressing a related concern, Walzer (1983) writes:

> For most children, parental choice almost certainly means less diversity, less tension, less opportunity for personal change than they would find in schools to which they were politically assigned. (219)

To the extent that choice initiatives protect privileged groups or deny all students exposure to alternative perspectives, they may limit a community's progress and pursuit of democratic community.[9]

   Democratic communitarians might be pleased that concern regarding isolation and segregation is part of the reason many mainstream analysts propose public school choice. These advocates (see, for example, Metz, 1990; Meier, 1991) suggest that regulated choice programs can diminish the isolation of a community's subgroups, but that unregulated school choice threatens "further segregation of students along well-entrenched lines of class, race, gender, and handicapping convention" (Bastian, 1990, 181).

Magnet programs, for example, have been used to promote racial integration. They are publicly financed and administered alternatives to traditional school settings. Participation in them is voluntary. These schools or programs within schools typically have special features (a particular academic focus, an alternative pedagogic orientation, extra funding, and so on) that attract students. Their popularity creates a large pool of applicants, which permits selection criteria that can create a diverse student population. These programs often are used to lessen middle class and white flight from city schools and as a part of a district's desegregation efforts (Metz, 1990). Some democratic communitarians might argue that these programs do more than simply desegregate. They help students identify common interests that transcend some of the racial and class divisions that often stunt a community's growth.

Other democratic communitarians might not be convinced. Factors beyond a student's race, gender, or ethnicity often determine admission into magnet programs. In fact, although magnet programs often achieve racial and ethnic diversity, limited space frequently leaves "black and Hispanic students, low-income students, students with low-achievement, students with absence and behavior problems, handicapped students, and limited-English-proficient students [with little access to magnet programs]" (Moore and Davenport, 1990, 188; also see Carnegie Foundation for the Advancement of Teaching, 1992). In addition, these programs commonly are charged with creaming—accepting only students with the best skills or those easiest to teach, and leaving students and teachers in traditional schools even more isolated than they were initially (see, for example, *New York Times*, 1991a; *Los Angeles Times*, 1992). Democratic communitarians might be particularly troubled by Moore and Davenport's findings:

> In the [public] school systems that we studied [New York City, Chicago, Philadelphia, and Boston], school choice schemes have become a new form of segregation, . . . based on race, income level, and previous school performance. (Moore and Davenport, 1990, 189)

In short, magnet programs will not fully integrate a district. Depending on their design, however, they may help. Studies of a school choice plan's impact on student segregation would be of central importance to democratic communitarians.

2. *Will a given school choice proposal increase or decrease the number of interests students consciously share?* Increasingly, classroom diversity mirrors that of the nation. Those committed to the value of strong communities worry that bonds among students have weakened as the population has become more diverse, the number of shared values and goals in neighborhood schools has lessened, and the emphasis on individual rights and goals has grown (Grant, 1988). Currently, students choose without hesitation to compete for grades, admission to college, and other marks of status. They rarely come together to determine goals that they then pursue collectively. As a result, schools reflect and reinforce our culture's emphasis on individualism.

The absence of communal experiences in schools and the orientation toward individual advancement might be termed a crisis by democratic communitarians, but it strikes neither mainstream policy analysts nor the public as cause for concern. This, perhaps more than anything else, demonstrates the marginal status of democratic communitarian priorities.

Does school choice provide democratic communitarians with a way to respond? Mary Anne Raywid (1987) believes choice has the potential to help educators establish communities with shared interests and strong interpersonal bonds:

> Choice yields a student body whose members are alike in some educationally important way—perhaps a shared interest, a common learning style, or a preference for a certain type of school climate. When choice is extended to teachers, it yields a faculty with a common philosophy of education and shared values. The outcome is a widely shared ethos, which makes group cohesion and a stronger sense of affiliation with the school more likely for all. (767)

Choice can increase the number of interests students consciously share, by permitting parents and students to select schools with specific identities, pedagogical styles, and curricular priorities. In addition, the commonalty of interests fostered by school choice may strengthen bonds between students by fostering motivation for collective undertakings that focus on common interests. In schools where students share interests, they also may be more likely to identify with one another and to form interpersonal bonds that transcend class, race, gender, and other common divisions. The potential contribution of such arrangements toward democratic communitarian goals is substantial.

But is a shared interest in science, the arts, or the media sufficient to promote democratic and communal interactions? Probably not. An enormous difference exists between settings in which individual students happen to have the same goals and interests, and those in which interests are shared. A shared interest is the product of democratic deliberation. It is an interest that reflects community members' understanding of and commitment to one another's priorities and needs.

A whole class of students might desire careers as scientists, for example, but this arrangement on its own does little to combat prevailing cultural norms of individualism and competition. It does not necessarily lead to a process that helps students transcend narrow understandings of self-interest. It does not necessarily help students recognize their interdependence or lead to the collective pursuit of shared goals. "How many premeds does it take to screw in a light bulb?" a familiar joke goes. "Five. One to put the bulb in place and four to pull the ladder out from below."

A college setting in which dozens of students with similar interests struggle to learn similar material may provide the opportunity for collective undertakings and strong interpersonal bonds. It also may ease the development of shared interests, but this outcome is far from assured. In the case of premeds, highly competitive admissions standards and cut-throat cultural norms often create what democratic communitarians would consider a dysfunctional community. In other cases, status hierarchies and divisions, reflecting athletic ability, looks, grades, race, class, gender, and numerous other factors, combine to make social cohesion difficult even among individuals who choose to attend the same school or program.

Moreover, schools with particular orientations may facilitate communal experiences, but they may not lead students to form strong bonds or to make meaningful connections with those in more diverse public arenas. If, for example, students come to believe that only commonality (interest, gender, religion, etc.) makes collective efforts possible, school choice may retard the growth of truly democratic communities—communities that recognize that their strength lies in their ability to capitalize on their diversity.

Still, school choice plans may offer educators with democratic communitarian goals more opportunities for success than they might otherwise have. To be effective, educators committed to fostering shared interests would need to develop pedagogy and curriculum that transcend divisions and help foster democratic and communal settings. An educational culture would have to be created where students worked together toward goals they collectively determined. The ability of school choice to further this agenda is far from clear. Hopefully, however, it is clear that if democratic communitarians debated school choice initiatives, their discussions would raise issues that currently get little systematic attention.

HUMANISTIC PSYCHOLOGISTS' RESPONSES TO MODERN CHOICE INITIATIVES

Humanistic psychologists, like mainstream analysts, would be deeply troubled by the constraining bureaucracy that often results from direct democratic control. For this, as well as for other reasons, they might support school choice. At the same time, some analysts with humanistic commitments would doubt the desirability of this policy direction. Although the outcome of discussions among humanists is uncertain, it is clear that their assessments of school choice would spark debates that are markedly different from current policy discussions.

Choice as a System of Governance—Reactions of Humanistic Psychologists

For humanists, the desirable features of governance through choice are clear. Humanists want the freedom to engage students in a broad and highly personalized curriculum and they believe that students should take a major role in guiding their studies. Ideally, writes Carl Rogers (1977),

> The student develops his own program of learning, alone or in co-operation with others. Exploring his own interests, facing this wealth of resources, he makes the choices as to his own learning direction. (14)

School choice can support this process. As schools work to attract students, they may become more attentive to students' interests than traditional public schools were. In addition, market arrangements may permit students and parents to select from a range of different educational environments. Students might pick a school that emphasizes math and science, one focused on literature, or one that explores public policy. Alternatively, they might select a school with a teaching style they find appealing.

Humanists also might join with choice advocates and support this reform, believing that it would bring fewer regulations than centralized governance systems. The current system of direct democratic control through school boards creates forums in which numerous parties compete to shape educators' priorities and practices. Outcomes that matter to business leaders, community organizations, and other interest groups get substantial attention—often much more than the goals of individual students. As Carl Rogers wrote in the early 1980s:

> The schools are, to a degree never seen before, regulated from outside. State-designated curricula, federal and state laws, and bureaucratic regulations, intrude on every classroom and school activity. The teacher–student relationship is easily lost in a confusing web of rules, limits, and required "objectives." (1983, 11–12)

For a related set of reasons, humanistic psychologists would reject the system of governance desired by democratic communitarians. Humanistic psychologists believe that educational priorities should reflect the concerns of particular students, not broad goals for the group. They would worry that attempts by well-meaning school boards to align educational practice with community concerns would limit teachers' ability to respond to the particular needs and interests of individual students. The school board meeting, which excited democratic communitarians, would threaten humanistic psychologists.

Despite these reasons to support school choice, some humanistic educators might be hesitant to promote these initiatives. Careful analysis of choice advocates' proposals to create an educational marketplace reveals demands for something less than a free market. Proponents of choice want to free educators to choose different educational approaches, but they grant less latitude when the discussion turns to the ends of education. School choice advocates believe that market pressures will foster "better" schools. These advocates neither want nor anticipate that choice will lead to the creation of schools that adopt widely varying aims. The plan laid out in *America 2000*, for example, talks of providing "flexibility in exchange for accountability" (Department of Education, 1991, 2) and President Clinton (1994) put out a similar message. He supports varied forms of public school choice so long as students learn "what they need to know to compete and win in the global economy" (A9). The founding director of 24 alternative schools in New York City's District 4 explains:

> State boards of education have the right to say, "These are the outcomes we want." But it's up to schools and districts to develop the strategies to get those outcomes. (Fliegel, in Brandt, 1990/91b, 24)

In fact, a broad coalition of educators and politicians hope to institute standards, tests, curriculum frameworks, and report cards on results.

They aim to provide the guidelines by which parents can measure the success of their children's school and others can discuss both the quality and equality of the educational system (Department of Education, 1991; also see National Council on Education Standards and Testing, 1992).

Such standards seem likely to constrain development of the kind of schools humanistic psychologists champion. Humanists want schools that respect students' diverse needs and interests, especially those which extend beyond the kind of academic skills and occupational concerns reflected in state and national goals.

Student Experience and School Choice—Reactions of Humanistic Psychologists

Chubb and Moe base their call for school choice on the following summary of the need for educational reform:

> [T]he schools are failing in their core academic mission, particularly in the more rigorous areas of study—math, science, foreign languages—so crucial to a future of sophisticated technology and international competition. America's children are not learning enough, they are not learning the right things, and, most debilitating of all, they are not learning how to learn. (Chubb and Moe, 1990, 1)

This rhetoric reveals the distance between the mainstream priorities that drive choice initiatives and the concerns of psychological humanists. Policy analysts hoping to promote self-actualization would reject Chubb and Moe's analytic assumptions and, more fundamentally, the goals they associate with school quality.

"Where," they would ask, "is the student's voice in this mainstream call for reform?" This policy talk reflects the mainstream focus on what Maslow (1968a) calls "extrinsic learning, i.e., learning of the outside, learning of the impersonal" (691). Rather than considering students' needs and interests, Chubb and Moe define "the core academic mission" in terms of its relation to "the future of sophisticated technology and international competition" (1). Their narrow emphasis on cognitive development would trouble humanistic educators, and the privileged status they accord economic goals would be viewed as cause for alarm. This rhetoric downplays the significance of students' developmental needs, their diverse academic, vocational, and artistic interests, and their role in guiding the educational process. As a result, even if humanists accepted the claim that choice would promote an institutional context conducive to the school characteristics researchers associate with "effective schools," they still might be hesitant to support this reform.

From a humanistic perspective, the school characteristics and academic outcomes associated with "effective schools" are uncertain indicators of a quality education. The substantial body of literature known as "effective schools research" (see Purkey and Smith, 1983, for a review) identifies the characteristics of schools in which students do particularly well on measures of academic achievement. These include clear goals, high academic expectations, order and discipline, homework, strong leadership, school site management, and parent involvement. Such features may promote modest gains in achievement, but this model takes neutral stands on matters of great importance to humanistic psychologists. To say that a school has "clear goals" or "strong leadership," for example, says little about the values that guide its students and teachers. Are these "clear goals" narrow and utilitarian or do they reflect a commitment to what humanistic educators might call the "whole child"? Are order and discipline achieved through external rewards and sanctions (grades, detentions, conditioned deference to authority) or do they result from intrinsically motivated students? School choice may promote "effective schools," but humanists want different, not more efficient, education. Choice advocates present no evidence that their policies will lead to the kinds of student experiences humanistic educators desire.

The relevance of these concerns becomes clearer when one realizes that roughly 85% of schools of choice are religious schools and many of the remaining 15% are elite private schools. These schools may have clear goals, strong leaders, order, discipline, and a number of other attributes that foster scholastic achievement—but both anecdotal and empirical evidence suggests that they often fall short on many matters of prime concern to humanistic educators. Many of these settings are authoritarian, elitist, constraining, and at times abusive (see, for example, McLaren, 1986; Crosier, 1991). More generally, as Walzer (1983) points out, the relative homogeneity of private and parochial schools may provide students with a narrow rather than a broadening educational experience.

Relatively few private schools make a full commitment to humanistic values. As John Goodlad (1978), the former dean of UCLA's school of education, writes, "When people come from abroad and ask me to send them . . . to a humanistic school I am hard pressed to recommend one" (19).

This is not to say that private or parochial schools completely neglect humanistic concerns. In fact, much of the attraction to private schools stems from the personal attention they provide students and from their willingness to accommodate individual differences (see Raywid, 1985; Kraushaar, 1972, 7). Strikingly, humanistic concerns, though the exception when policy analysts discuss the desirability of choice systems, frequently appear when advocates seek to illustrate the desirability of choice by describing exemplary schools. The 1990/91 issue of *Educational Leadership*, for example, includes numerous portraits of successful schools of choice. In these discussions, the values of humanistic psychologists are well represented.

Launa Ellison, for instance, describes the Minneapolis school in which she teaches. Every September in this K–8 school, a student, his or her parents, and a teacher meet to

> discuss the student's strengths, interests, and needs, including academic, physical, interpersonal, and artistic goals. Together they choose specific goals for the student, going beyond traditional curriculum. (Ellison, 1990/91, 37)

Similarly, Deborah Meier (implementor of the most commonly cited successful choice/magnet program) writes that she aimed at creating "a terrifically exciting school," and at another point she comments, "You want a school small enough so everyone can see each other's work, hear each other's viewpoint." She wants students to know that they "can make something of the world because it's an interesting place to figure out, and that life is meant to be enjoyed" (in Goldberg, 1990/91, 27). Her rhetoric embodies the concerns of psychological humanists (as well as those of democratic communitarians) far more than it does those of utilitarians and rights theorists. Meier did not write that she wanted her school to compete favorably with other schools in the district. Note, in particular, her attitude toward the use of standardized test scores as a means of assessing the effectiveness of particular educational environments. "The kids read and write, and they talk and they're clearly growing. My kids are doing well. . . . The test scores are fine in some schools where I know they're not learning anything" (27).

In short, it is not clear whether school choice will further a humanistic agenda. Are schools that students and parents choose more attentive to humanistic concerns than neighborhood schools are, or are these schools selected for other reasons? Would school choice make it more likely that students' educational experiences will align with their interests and their full range of needs? Systematic consideration of such questions is clearly possible, but it is not undertaken by analysts who debate school choice. Mainstream assessments of school choice focus on efficiency and equity—cognitive measures of success are taken as unproblematic proxies for quality.

Implementation Issues for Humanistic Policy Analysts

Given the chance, would parents and students select schools with an emphasis on humanistic concerns? Currently, analysts ignore this question. They focus on whether various choice proposals ensure equal access to "good" schools, not on the conceptions of quality that guide the choices of students and parents.[10]

Although the data are sketchy, it does seem clear that many parents and students, when assessing the quality of their school system, do not rely on humanistic criteria—particularly when assessing high schools. This places humanists in an awkward, if ironic, position. Humanists believe that individuals should be freed to direct their own education. Nonetheless, when given the chance, it seems that many students and parents do not select schools that provide students with the kind of pedagogic and curricular freedom humanists endorse. While school choice initiatives might enable the creation of schools that embody humanistic goals and processes, much of this potential seems likely to go unrealized.

Humanistic educators hoping to use choice to further their agenda would search for ways to respond. Clearly, part of their project would involve convincing parents, students, and educators of the desirability of their form of education. With this goal in mind, some humanistically oriented policy analysts and advocates have undertaken studies that examine the effects of humanistic education. Carl Rogers describes these studies in *Freedom to Learn for the 80's* in a chapter he titles "What Are the Facts?" These studies suggest that students

> learn more, attend school more often (financially important), are more creative, more capable of problem solving, when the teacher provides the kind of human, facilitative climate [he recommends]. (Rogers, 1983, 197)

Although some of these studies emphasize humanistic goals, most assess the impact of humanistic education on mainstream understandings of quality education. Rogers (1983) explains that studies with this focus are important because they provide "the hard data that administrators and executives seek" (197). However, by implying that the value of humanistic educational strategies can be tied to their impact on cognitive gains, Rogers and others who make this argument set a dangerous precedent. This approach permits mainstream critics of humanistic education to dismiss humanistic practices by citing studies that indicate that humanistic practices are uncertain means to cognitive gains. Moreover, it may undermine humanists' broader goal of reframing notions of "quality" education.

A related dilemma also puts humanistic educators in a difficult position. Much of students' and parents' hesitancy to endorse humanistic goals stems from appreciation of the importance of school credentials and standardized measures of cognitive performance. Such criteria often regulate students' future opportunities. Consequently, at the same time that advocates of humanistic education need to point out the dangers of a narrow academic focus, they also must find ways to reduce the vulnerability of students who select their programs. As Delpit (1988) points out, this danger is particularly significant for poor and minority students for whom schools offer much-needed access to what she terms the "culture of power."

Thus, humanists' problems with assessment connect to their problems with recruitment. To the extent that humanists remain true to their goals, their methods of assessment may lack the formally objective criteria and cognitive/academic orientation that are needed to convince students and parents to choose humanistic schools. As a result, parents and students may avoid humanistic schools, fearing that this educational plan will place them at a disadvantage in the competitive arena they may want to enter after school. In short, although humanists want to free students to pursue their own educational priorities, it is unclear that such freedom will lead many to select humanistic approaches to education when faced with structural incentives to emphasize academic priorities.

More could be said about these dilemmas and their implications for humanistic policy analysis. For now it is enough to note that choice initiatives lead humanists to ask different questions than mainstream analysts. Those in the mainstream struggle to design choice initiatives that are "responsive, productive, cost-efficient, and equitable" (Cibulka, 1990, 58). Humanists strive to make humanistic schools an attractive choice.

CONCLUDING THOUGHTS

Policy analysts must consider numerous options when they assess choice initiatives. Should public monies fund students who go to private schools? Should these funds go to religious schools? Should students be allowed to select schools in other districts? Should publicly funded schools be allowed to have selective admissions procedures? Should private schools be allowed to use vouchers as partial payments and require students to supplement the vouchers to meet tuition requirements?

When responding to these questions, mainstream analysts do not all come to the same conclusions, but they do base their judgments on similar ethical criteria. Concern for utility, equity, and human capital development structure both the form and focus of their analysis.

Democratic communitarians, in contrast, focus on the relationships that characterize the group. They ask whether various school choice proposals are likely to promote strong communal ties that provide students with support, affirmation, a sense of belonging, and a sense of direction. They also consider the degree to which these plans help students appreciate the importance of collective action and reflection. In addition, they wonder if students' school experiences provide them with the skills and motivation to work toward democratic communities after they graduate. Finally, they consider whether school choice will foster or hinder social integration. Some might argue that controlled choice plans can foster settings in which a diverse student body forms learning communities. Some might worry that choice will increase the degree to which privileged students insulate themselves from the pulls of common agendas that reflect the needs, priorities, and perspectives of diverse populations.

Democratic communitarians also would evaluate school boards and free market governance arrangements differently than many mainstream analysts would. Their hesitancy to endorse market mechanisms extends beyond their concern for efficiency and equity. They would view free markets as costly because they isolate decision makers and bypass opportunities for the community to collectively develop a shared "apprehension of a common good [education]" (see Kaufman-Osborn, 1985, 846).

Humanistic educators also would assess school choice proposals differently than their mainstream counterparts would. Mainstream assessments of school choice initiatives consider whether these changes in governance will make schools more responsive to the priorities of parents and students. Embedded in their analysis, however, are assumptions regarding the nature of these priorities. Student achievement on academic measures dominates these analysts' conceptions of quality education. In addition, they understand a fair choice system to be one in which all students have the same opportunity to master academic material and gain admission to a prestigious college.

Humanistic educators would reject this narrow emphasis on equity and excellence. Rather than focusing on mainstream concerns, they would ask whether humanistic priorities are as marginal in the schools that students and parents select as they are in the ones to which students are assigned.

School choice clearly provides humanistic psychologists with an opportunity to advance their agenda. The outcome, however, remains uncertain. Humanists would therefore consider ways to structure choice policies so as to enable the creation of humanistic schools. They also would work to convince policy analysts and the public at large of the value of humanistic educational approaches. Finally, once the case for their alternative orientation is made, they would work to develop meaningful ways to assess performance. As Aaron Wildavsky (1987) notes, "Educators who continually say that they deal with the whole child apparently feel that they are not responsible for any particular part" (323). To gain the support of the public and the policy community, humanistic psychologists need to develop a compelling response to this criticism.

7
The Eight-Year Study: Evaluating Progressive Education

Suppose that the goals of educational policy and practice were to change. Suppose that practitioners and policy analysts were to develop and assess schools that aimed to embody communitarian and humanistic priorities. Chapters 5 and 6 considered the changes these orientations imply for two specific policy debates. What if the focus were on transforming entire schools rather than on particular policy proposals? What might happen if practitioners and analysts committed to these alternative agendas were given the financial resources to move from thought to action? How different would their schools be and how might analysts assessed them?

In 1930 a group of the nation's leading educators came together to discuss the untapped potential of progressive educational practices. They were frustrated that progressive pedagogy and curriculum rarely were found in high schools. The chief obstacle, they believed, was college admission standards that emphasized particular academic courses and unit requirements. While recognizing the value of academic disciplines, progressive educators often found these requirements constraining.

THREE QUESTIONS

If educators and students were freed from these unit requirements, could they create "democracy's high school" (Aiken, 1942a, 41)? While pursuing this goal, could they turn schools into places where "the common problems of American youth become the heart of the curriculum" (57)? And if students pursued these alternative goals in high school, would they succeed in college?

These were the questions that motivated the Commission on the

119

Relation of School and College to embark on the Eight-Year Study. The Carnegie, Rockefeller, and other foundations contributed over one million dollars to the Progressive Education Association (PEA) in search of an answer (Redefer, 1950, 33). Thirty schools (fifteen private, fifteen public) and two school districts (Denver and Tulsa) participated in the study.[1] To enable experimentation, those conducting the study convinced over 300 colleges and universities (virtually all selective colleges and universities) to wave standard course and unit requirements for applicants from these schools.

The PEA hoped to support and monitor this effort in two ways. First, the PEA employed teams of noted curriculum specialists to work with local educators and to document their practices. In addition, a staff of evaluators led by Ralph Tyler (a pioneer in the field of educational evaluation) monitored the impact of these alternative programs on students. These evaluators created and implemented numerous measures of the schools' alternative goals. They assessed, for example, the degree to which these schools fostered "democratic character." In addition, in an effort to determine the impact of this alternative approach on college performance, 1,475 students in these alternative programs were paired with nonparticipants who attended the same college, were of the same age, sex, and race, had the same scholastic aptitude scores, and came from similar homes and communities. These pairs of students were followed and sporadically interviewed throughout their college careers. Records of their academic performance, their attitudes toward school and life, and their participation in extracurricular activities also were analyzed and compared. The study, which lasted 8 years, became the largest social science experiment of its day.

WHY LOOK AT THE EIGHT-YEAR STUDY?

For the most part, those discussing school choice, tracking, and other policy issues fail to pay systematic attention to democratic communitarian and humanistic goals. One can note this omission, but there are limits to the amount of inquiry that can be done on what might be termed a "policy silence" (see Tyack and Hansot, 1988). How much can be said about policy arguments that are rarely advanced? How certain can one be about the arguments those with an alternative focus might make? Broad commentary is certainly possible, but what about specific details—the particulars of policy and practice. And even if we speculate on some of the goals these educators might pursue, how much can we say about the likely outcomes of these efforts and about the ways in which mainstream analysts might respond?

The alternative goals pursued in this experiment, its scale, and its prominence as an effort at educational reform, all make the Eight-Year Study a rare and valuable source of data. It was a large and path-breaking effort to put forward democratic communitarian and humanistic goals. Indeed, the compatibility of the study's rhetoric with the perspectives outlined in Chapters 3 and 4 is striking. "Almost without exception," Giles, McCutchen, and Zechiel (1942) explain in their survey of the curricular changes that took place,

> schools of the Eight-year Study accept these two fundamental assumptions. . . . The educational program must *meet the needs of adolescents* and seek to *preserve and extend democracy as a way of life.* (5, emphasis in original)

To explain their orientation, they quoted a passage from the PEA's report *Science in General Education:*

> The purpose of general education is to meet the needs of individuals . . . in such a way as to promote the fullest possible realization of personal potentialities and the most effective participation in a democratic society. (quoted in Giles, McCutchen, & Zechiel, 1942, 85)

The PEA published five volumes (over 2,100 pages) to document the changes that occurred in the schools and their effects. Examination of this literature permits consideration of how adoption of an alternative set of goals can transform both educational practice and the form and content of evaluation and policy analysis.

In addition, the grand nature of this experiment makes reactions to it particularly revealing. Frequently, educators' attempts to pursue alternative agendas exist only on the margins of the policy arena. Mainstream analysts may note these undertakings, but they generally receive only superficial, if somewhat positive, attention. The size of the Eight-Year Study, the bold nature of its goals, as well as the involvement of prominent schools, elite students, and leading educational researchers, all made it difficult for the mainstream policy community to either miss or dismiss its findings. A consideration of their reactions—the criticisms, the silences, and the points of praise—may help clarify the forces shaping, constraining, and organizing mainstream policy rhetoric.

Below, I discuss the study's goals and design in greater detail, describe the educational manifestations of this vision, and consider the innovative methods used to assess students in these programs. I then evaluate the reactions of the mainstream educational policy community to this study and its findings.

UNDERLYING COMMITMENTS TO DEMOCRATIC COMMUNITARIAN AND HUMANISTIC PRIORITIES

The Commission on the Relation of School and College was created in October 1930. The 26 members included teachers, professors, principals, college presidents, admissions officers, evaluators, educational philosophers, and journalists.[2] Commission members shared the belief that "secondary education in the United States did not have a clear-cut, definite, central purpose" (Aiken, 1942a, 4). They felt that schooling practices were largely a function of convention rather than reflection. They believed that these practices aligned poorly with students' particular needs and those of the society they were to join. These reformers wanted to clearly define the purpose of education, reach a common understanding of the current shortcomings, and then devise ways to respond.

After a year of study, the Commission produced a statement identifying 18 "areas which needed exploration and improvement" (Aiken, 1942a, 4). Their critique demonstrated their commitment to humanistic and democratic priorities. Like Rogers (1983), Maslow (1968a), and other humanistic educators, members of the Commission worried that "the student's concerns were not taken into account" and that "the classroom was formal and completely dominated by the teacher." As a result, "the conventional high school curriculum was far removed from the real concerns of youth" (Aiken, 1942a, 6–7).

Commission members' commitment to democratic community is ably summarized by their statement that "our secondary schools did not prepare [students] adequately for the responsibilities of community life." They also found that

> little effort was made to lead youth into a clear understanding of the ideals of democracy [and] not many [students] had developed any strong sense of social responsibility or deep concern for the common welfare. (Aiken, 1942a, 4–5)

> Youth knew its rights and privileges, but often missed the rich significance of duty done and responsibilities fully met. Unselfish devotion to great causes was not a characteristic result of secondary education. (Aiken, 1942a, 10)

For similar reasons they worried when "[o]nly here and there did the Commission find principals who conceived of their work in terms of democratic leadership of the community, teachers, and students" (Aiken, 1942a, 9–10).

In short, Commission members wanted educational processes that reflected the needs and interests of youth and, at the same time, they wanted to train students in ways that would make them conscious of and responsive to social needs.

These reformers also were deeply concerned with students' academic progress. They worried, for example, that "the high school seldom challenged the student of first-rate ability to work up to the level of his intellectual powers" (Aiken, 1942a, 5) and that "most high school graduates were not competent in the use of the English language" (8). Their position on many seemingly mainstream concerns, however, often reflected their democratic communitarian and humanistic orientation. They complained, for example, that "teachers were not well equipped for their responsibilities." Rather than focusing on the teachers' training in academic disciplines, however, Commission members expressed the humanistic concern that teachers "lacked full knowledge of the nature of youth—of physical, intellectual, and emotional drives and growth." They also worried that "teachers seldom had any clear conception of democracy as a way of living which should characterize the whole life of the school" (Aiken, 1942a, 9). Similarly, these critics were concerned that "principals and teachers labored earnestly ... but usually without any comprehensive evaluation of the results of their work." Again, however, they emphasized an alternative set of concerns. Teachers and principals

> knew what grades students made on tests of knowledge and skill, but few knew or seemed really to care whether other objectives such as understandings, appreciations, clear thinking, social sensitivity, genuine interests were being achieved. (Aiken, 1942a, 10)

FROM THEORETICAL COMMITMENTS TO PRACTICE

> In the fall of 1933, the schools began planning for change. The Directing Committee had decided that the independence and autonomy of each school must be carefully guarded. . . . [It agreed to] render every possible assistance sought by the schools, but to avoid any tendency to dictate thought or action. (Aiken, 1942a, 15)

As a result, both the degree of change and the direction of change varied. Differing local priorities, site leadership, and contextual constraints (such as financial resources, pressures from parents, trustee priorities, and traditions) led to a wide range of experiences. Not surprisingly, the approach taken in a private school with 30 teachers and 300 students was often different from that taken in a city school with 80 teachers and 2,500 students (see Aiken, 1942a, 28). Still, the schools' common orientation, their sharing of ideas, and the centralized support they received from the PEA often led them to adopt similar goals and comparable organizational and curricular strategies.

In the vast majority of cases educators from the 30 schools focused on what I have called humanistic and democratic communitarian priorities. They wanted to engage students with curriculum that (1) reflected students' interests and the particular needs of youth, and (2) provided students with the skills and social orientation needed to further the democratic process. As Aiken explained, "Two forces unite[d] to determine the curriculum . . . the demands of the society and the concerns of adolescents" (74).

For these reformers, responding to such demands was the essence of democratic education. In fact, they understood democratic education to combine attention to the priorities of humanistic psychologists and democratic communitarians. One crucial modification to the humanistic perspective makes this synthesis possible. Like Dewey, these reformers rejected humanists' claim that the potentials to be realized have their base somewhere deep in the individual and that one discovers one's true nature by stripping away the influence of society. Instead of trying to negate the influence of social forces, they argued that

> a distinctive personality cannot be developed in isolation. It develops only when there is free interplay with other personalities. . . . While wholesome individual development is the basic goal, associated living is the better means of achieving it. (University School, Ohio State University, 1942, 720)

In short, educators in Ohio and in most of the participating schools understood democratic education to require dual commitments to humanistic and democratic communitarian ethical priorities.

A Public School System Example: Tulsa, Oklahoma

Tulsa's adaptation of the progressive priorities was relatively typical. To help clarify the kinds of curricular and organizational changes brought about by this experiment, I highlight six features of the program.

Small Schools and Schools Within Schools. It is important to note from the outset that only a portion of students in most of the public schools participated in the study.[3] Participation often was limited to students of average or above-average academic ability. This decision is partially explained by the Commission's desire to assess students' performance in college. Students with below-average academic skills rarely went to college. The small size of these programs also may have made it easier to coordinate the changes and to develop coherent communities of students and teachers. In Tulsa 200 tenth-grade "accelerated" students were selected by their ninth-grade teachers to participate in the experiment. They spent 3 hours each day in the "block," where they studied "social relations" (problems confronting tenth-grade boys and girls) for 2 hours and spent 1 hour involved in either physical education or a creative activity such as music, woodworking, auto mechanics, or art. They then spent 3 hours taking electives.

Common School Goals. Given the schools' new direction, explicit and thoughtful consideration of their alternative goals was very important. Most schools created committees of teachers and sometimes students, which set the school's priorities. In Tulsa, a steering committee was formed to address this concern. Their goals were (1) "to develop those attitudes, skills, and understandings which will enable the individual, as a member of the social group concerned, to become a positive force in the process of achievement of the democratic ideal," and (2) "to develop an effective personality through an understanding of self, and through an appreciation of the importance of the aesthetic and the spiritual in human activities" (Giles, McCutchen, and Zechiel, 1942, 93).

A Core Curriculum. The committee then developed a core curriculum based on these priorities. This curriculum was to "meet the general education needs of all secondary school pupils and should be required of all pupils" (Giles, McCutchen, and Zechiel, 1942, 94).[4] Participating students were assigned for 3 hours each day to core classrooms. In these classes students addressed topics in an interdisciplinary manner and explored the significance of each issue for both individuals and the society. During a tenth-grade unit on health, for example, students focused on questions that included, "How do the different parts of my body work?" and "How does the community help me to keep well?" (Giles, McCutchen, and Zechiel, 1942, 336; Tulsa High Schools, 1942, 645). In addition, both practical and theoretical questions were studied. During a unit on democracy, students were asked to consider how "democratic ideals and principles affected the history of government and political activities in the United States" and the question, "How may I participate in government itself to promote processes of desirable evolutionary change?" (Giles, McCutchen, and Zechiel, 1942, 336).

Teacher/Pupil Planning. Once the core curricular goals were specified, a process they referred to as teacher/pupil planning was brought into play. This procedure was used in Tulsa and elsewhere to strengthen the alignment of students' interests and needs with curricular content.

Reports on this strategy from both evaluators and teachers indicate that teachers encountered difficulties when they began using this approach, but that teacher/pupil planning proved to be a very effective way to bring democracy into the classroom. They found this process enhanced students' sense of self-worth and led students to take greater responsibility for their own education. It also provided students with an opportunity to work collectively, under the supervision of the teacher, to reach decisions that reflected the varied interests and priorities of group members.

Given the many conceptions of pupil "empowerment" that appear in literature on educational democracy, it is important to note that these schools pursued *teacher*/pupil planning, not pupil planning. Although students played an important role in shaping the ways in which topics were explored, they did not control the process. The broad learning objectives were set by teachers and administrators. The specific curricular content was influenced by students' interests, but also by "the uniqueness of the local community, [by teachers' assessments of students' needs], and [by] the strengths and weaknesses of the teacher" (Giles, McCutchen, and Zechiel, 1942, 77). Ultimately, classroom teachers decided what would be taught.[5]

Workplace Democracy. Just as the pursuit of democratic classrooms led teachers to greatly increase students' role in classroom decision making, attempts to promote democratic leadership in schools greatly increased the role teachers played in determining educational goals and in selecting policies to further those goals. In schools and districts where course content previously had been determined by superintendents and principals, faculty committees now played the leading role. In some schools all decisions that affected the school were discussed by the faculty or by faculty representatives. A few private schools created committees of teachers that helped draft budgets and determine teachers' salaries. Aiken (1942a) reports that "this more extensive participation in curriculum building, policy making, and school management adds to teachers' loads, but they [teachers] testify that it is worth much more in growth than it costs in time and energy" (42).

Experience-Based Pedagogy. Small schools, increased teacher decision-making authority, a core curriculum, and teacher/pupil planning were found in most of the schools. These organizational changes were often combined with a pedagogic commitment to active, experiential learning environments. Progressive educators were attracted to this approach because it motivated students, reflected student preferences, provided opportunities for students to work together toward goals they collectively determined, integrated subject matter, and tied academic discussions to practical concerns and community priorities.

At Tulsa's Will Rogers High School, for example, students in one class discussed possible topics of study among themselves and with teachers in their program. They decided to spend several weeks studying the conservation of natural resources. As the process of teacher/pupil planning continued, students considered their priorities and interests. One student explained,

> We not only wanted to be made aware of the problems and the need for conservation, but we also wanted to make others aware of this need. Not in some remote part of the United States but right here in our own community. Knowing that people are more impressed by what they actually see than what they read or hear, we decided to make a movie of conservation problems in the community in and around Tulsa. (in Giles, McCutchen, and Zechiel, 1942, 141–42)

The students then formed six committees, each with a different focus: conservation of soil, water conservation, flood control, wild life conservation, conservation of minerals, and forest conservation. Then, before beginning their study, the class considered the

> behavior patterns, or changes we wanted brought about in our personal attitudes and skills. These behavior patterns included learning to work together in groups with maximum of efficiency . . . learn[ing] cooperation in our work with each other [and learning] more about the problems facing our community. (a student, in Giles, McCutchen, and Zechiel, 1942, 141–42)

With these goals in mind, each committee researched its particular set of issues. In addition to using library materials to learn about geography, forestry, soil management, and so forth, the students requested and then examined reading material from various government departments. The students also gathered information by visiting sites where conservation was taking place. They then wrote reports, made class presentations, and received feedback from the class and the instructors. As a next step, each committee wrote a movie script discussing its particular topic. A committee of students then formed to integrate these segments. For the culminating activity, the class shot a movie at various locations, including the Grand River Dam, Lake Spavinaw, the C.C.C. camp at Broken Arrow, and Mohawk Park (Giles, McCutchen, and Zechiel, 1942, 141–43).

This kind of experience-based project was the ideal that these schools pursued and in many cases created—though clearly not on a daily basis. The attractiveness of this approach lay in the way it incorporated students' interests, examined a significant social issue, and helped develop students' ability to collectively pursue shared goals.

A Private School Example: Dalton

Because these experience-based projects reflected the environments in which the students lived, they took different forms in different communities. To provide a sense of this contrast, I describe a project that took place at the Dalton School, a private day school in New York City. Rather than placing the primary emphasis on social concerns, this project emphasized student emotional and creative growth as well as the development of important academic and life skills.

At Dalton, students did not passively discuss and reflect on childhood or talk about infant siblings; they worked in the school's nursery. Enrolled in a course titled "Nursery-Biology," each ninth-grade girl (Dalton's high school was then a school for girls) spent a week working from 8:45 till 3:00 in the nursery. For the rest of the semester the girls were "free to use the babies as an 'observation laboratory'" (Dalton Schools, 1942, 124).

Much of this curriculum focused on human biology in relation to the nursery. In addition to learning how to care for young children, students working in the nursery kept daily records of the babies' weight, temperature, and diet. They also studied issues relating to each child's health and physical development. This emphasis on scientific aspects of human biology was complemented by a focus on the social context of childhood in New York City. The students explored these issues by visiting the homes and the neighborhoods in which the children lived and by visiting institutions that serve children: New York Hospital, Borden Milk Plant, Yorkville Health Clinic, and the markets in Little Italy (see Dalton Schools, 1942, 125). Finally, the topics covered in the course extended beyond the immediate issues related to child care. For example, students discussed human reproduction, puberty, and sex taboos. In addition, "psychological factors in family life are observed on visits to the babies' homes, and are discussed in simple terms on return to the nursery" (Dalton Schools, 1942, 127).

As these examples illustrate, by engaging students in active, experience-based projects, educators at the 30 schools found they could more effectively pursue their primary goals. Students' needs and interests could help to shape the design of these endeavors. In addition, a democratic orientation and social mode of learning could be fostered by the content of the curriculum (students' exposure to real world issues and experiences) and by the collective and democratic ways the groups of students carried out these activities.

TRANSFORMING POLICY ANALYSIS AND EVALUATION BY MEASURING PERSONAL AND SOCIAL ADJUSTMENT AND SOCIAL SENSITIVITY

It is impossible to estimate the wastage which results from education's ignorance of the consequences of its efforts. (Aiken, 1942c, xix)

In many respects, the schools described above were innovative, relatively rare, and perhaps quite desirable. They were not, however, the first of their kind. Progressive high schools like this had been created before.

Why then the focus on the Eight-Year Study? Why did Lawrence Cremin (1961) write that this Commission "may well remain as the [Progressive Education] Association's abiding contribution to the development of American education" (251)? What justification did Ralph Tyler (1986/87) have for labeling the study one of "the five most significant curriculum events in the twentieth century" (36)?

Prior to the Eight-Year Study, those striving to create progressive high schools aimed to better serve the students in their classes. They may have recognized that they were part of a movement, but their primary goal was local. The Progressive Education Association's study, in contrast, was designed to transform educational practice in the United States. It wanted to move progressive approaches from the margins to the mainstream.

To accomplish this task, the architects of the Eight-Year Study recognized that they needed to create measures of educational outcomes that reflected their alternative priorities. They were concerned that educators, rather than measuring what they cared about, often cared about what they could measure:

> Because instruments of appraisal in [these alternative] areas have not been available, the teacher tends to neglect other objectives and to strive only for results that can be ascertained with relative ease and objectivity. (Aiken, 1942c, xviii)

By developing methods of policy analysis and evaluation that aligned with progressive educators' alternative priorities, these reformers hoped to provide incentives and direction that would lead practitioners to alter their practices.

The challenge they faced was substantial. Prior to the study, assessments of policy and of educational outcomes did not include systematic consideration of the goals these progressives valued. Rather than assessing the formation of democratic character or students' development, there was a

> universal emphasis upon the accumulation of credits for promotion, graduation, and admission to college . . . To pass a course [a student] must remember certain facts and show proficiency in certain skills. Therefore, remembering knowledge and practicing techniques for examinations become the purposes of education for pupils and teachers alike. (Aiken, 1942c, xvii)

If the need for new means of assessing school success was clear, however, the solution was not. Evaluators felt confident when assessing students' knowledge of particular subjects, students' academic skills, and the number of course credits they received. Could similarly satisfying methods be developed to assess the alternative goals that progressives emphasized? It was one thing to note that "unselfish devotion to great causes was not a characteristic result of secondary education" (1942a, 10), and quite another thing to measure in a systematic and convincing way the impact of pedagogy and curriculum on the development of democratic character among students.

I examine the study's strategy for evaluating personal adjustment and social sensitivity. In addition to describing the evaluation strategies, I assess the degree to which the methods provide meaningful measures of these alternative goals. I also consider the transformation these approaches imply for policy analysis. The story that unfolds demonstrates the complexity of the challenge. It also indicates that the norms and values embedded in the structure of policy analysis, not simply the focus, must change if humanistic and democratic goals are to be considered. Although I aim to show that these efforts did not reach their ambitious target, I also hope to clarify their considerable contribution.

The Definitions of Personal and Social Adjustment

The betterment of students' personal and social adjustment was a concern shared by the participating schools and the evaluation staff. To pursue this goal they needed to develop a "practicable means of appraising personal and social adjustment" (Sheviakov and Block, 1942, 349). The Commission's first task was to specify the understanding of these concepts. It defined personal adjustment

> as including the subjective feelings of the individual, such feelings of adequacy and inadequacy, personal happiness and unhappiness, the adjustive reactions of the individual, the presence or absence of inner conflicting tendencies. (Sheviakov and Block, 1942, 350)

Social adjustment was defined as "the adequacy and effectiveness of a person's interactions with other people [age-mates, older and younger people, those of the opposite sex]" (Sheviakov and Block, 1942, 350) as well as the alignment of an individual's values with those of the broader society.

For the most part, these definitions mirrored those provided in other parts of the study. However, the Commission's notion of personal and social adjustment departed from humanistic beliefs when it argued that "optimum adjustment may be thought of as a compromise between the individual and the group to which he belongs" (Sheviakov and Block, 1942, 353). As the Commission elaborated, it endorsed traditional communitarian commitments and adjustment to mainstream values, writing, for example, that "desirable adjustment" occurs when the individual can "integrate successfully" his or her personal qualities

> with those expectations or demands which are imposed on him by the group to which he belongs. . . . This context of feelings and behaviors must be evaluated in terms of the status of the individual (i.e., his age, sex, position in society, etc.). The same behavior may be evaluated differently . . . in a boy or a girl. (Sheviakov and Block, 1942, 354)

Thus, the Commission defined a well-adjusted person as one whose personal qualities do not conflict with social norms or traditions. It did not criticize the ways in which gender roles, for example, often constrain the development of boys and girls. In effect, it labeled "healthy" those who had learned to fit in.

Use of Tests That Tapped Interests and Preferences Rather Than Personal and Social Adjustment

The evaluators' definition of desirable adjustment did not altogether square with the measures they proposed. The tests developed by the Commission were far more descriptive than evaluative. These "evaluations" did not assess the desirability of a student's social and personal adjustment; thus the evaluators' definition of this concept was less consequential than it might otherwise have been.

At the heart of the tests was a student interest questionnaire. This form listed 300 activities that occur in schools. Students noted whether they liked, disliked, or were indifferent toward these activities. Both academic and nonacademic activities were included on these surveys. Some questions examined students' attitudes toward mathematics, biology, or physics. Other questions examined students' attitudes toward activities such as "copying papers to make them neat" (Sheviakov and Block, 1942, 366). Finally, some questions examined students' feelings regarding interpersonal relations. Students taking these tests were asked, for example, whether they liked, disliked, or were indifferent toward "hitting someone who has annoyed me very much" (Sheviakov and Block, 1942, 367). A student's score on these tests also could be compared with those of classmates.

These tests were a retreat from the original goal. They were clearly original and marked a significant departure from mainstream educational evaluation and measurement. However, while they provided detailed and systematic information on students' preferences, they failed to measure personal and social adjustment. When the Commission considered this challenge, it found "cogent reasons against beginning a program . . . centering on an attempt to determine whether the adjustment of an individual is desirable or not" (Sheviakov and Block, 1942, 352). No test, they wrote, could be sufficiently sensitive to an individual's context. Knowledge of this context was needed before an individual's acts of adjustment (behavior) could be assessed. Moreover, they noted, "even then [a judgment] is apt to be a value judgment" (Sheviakov and Block, 1942, 352). Since they could not provide reliable and valid measures of personal adjustment, they decided to focus instead on providing information that might be of "value to the counselor." These tests did "afford the opportunity to look at a student from a new angle," "point to directions which ought to be investigated," and, in combination with other information, suggest "remedial steps" (Sheviakov and Block, 1942, 396–97).

The limited focus of these tests may have reflected a kind of scientific integrity, but it also signaled a retreat. As the Commission redefined the nature of its evaluation, it weakened the evaluation's connection to policy analysis. The tests may help monitor students' comfort with and interest in various academic and nonacademic activities, but they do not permit judgments of personal and social adjustment. Moreover, these tests cannot be used to demonstrate that progressive techniques help students adjust to the society, and they fail to provide meaningful incentives for educators to shift their focus from mainstream concerns. Sheviakov and Block's chapter may be titled "Evaluation of Personal and Social Adjustment," but the authors do not deliver on this promise.

The Definitions of Social Sensitivity

The Commission was strongly committed to Dewey's vision of democracy as a way of life and to developing students' orientation toward social needs. As they worked to develop means of assessing the achievement of these goals, they decided that assessing students' "social sensitivity" was of prime importance. After extensive conversations with teachers, the evaluators identified six "major aspects of social sensitivity of concern to teachers in the thirty schools" (Taba and McGuire, 1942, 161):

> 1. Social thinking, e.g., the ability (a) to get significant meanings from social facts, (b) to apply social facts and generalizations to new problems, (c) to respond critically and discriminatingly to ideas and arguments. . . .
> 2. Social attitudes, beliefs, and values; e.g., the basic personal positions, feelings, and concerns toward social phenomena, institutions, and issues. . . .
> 3. Social awareness; that is, the range and quality of factors or elements perceived in a situation. . . .
> 4. Social interests as revealed by liking to engage in socially significant activities. . . .
> 5. Social information; that is, familiarity with facts and generalizations relevant to significant social problems. . . .
> 6. Skill in social action, involving familiarity with the techniques of social action as well as the ability to use them. (Taba and McGuire, 1942, 161)

The Measures of Social Sensitivity

With these goals in mind, a variety of tests were created. One test demanded that students assess the accuracy and appropriateness of using different social facts and generalizations to support or critique a given policy direction. A different test aimed to classify the students' beliefs on social issues. This test asked students to indicate their agreement, disagreement, or uncertainty with respect to more than 200 statements relating to six different social issues: democracy, economic relations, labor and unemployment, race, nationalism, and militarism.

I will focus on a third and relatively representative kind of test. Students taking this exam were presented with a problematic situation and required to select one of three possible courses of action. They then chose justifications for this action from a list of "reasons." For example, students might read a brief description of the connection between working in mines and factories and the development of debilitating health conditions. They were told that improving these conditions could be quite expensive and then asked, "What should be done about such problems?" (Taba and McGuire, 1942, 180).

Students chose from one of three possible courses of action. The first, which the answer key tells us reflects "undemocratic" values, is to let the mine and factory owners decide what to do. The second, the "democratic" answer, is to have the government set "minimum standards for general working conditions." And the third, labeled a compromise, is to have joint committees of workers and employers make suggestions regarding improvements. Students then reviewed 20 reasons that might or might not support the stance they took. They chose the reasons they would use to support the course of action they already selected. Those scoring this part of the test noted both whether the reasons selected were consistent with the course of action proposed and whether these reasons reflected democratic values, undemocratic values, or rationalizations. One possible reason, for example, is, "Without regulation, business can be depended upon to make necessary improvements." This answer is said to reflect undemocratic values and to be consistent with the first and third courses of action (see Taba and McGuire, 1942, 181, for sample test questions and answers).

This test aims to answer three kinds of questions. First, how broadly does the pupil relate principles or value generalizations to chosen courses of action? Second, can the student construct well-reasoned arguments? The test measures "the percent of the total number of reasons checked by the student which are inconsistent with the course of action chosen," the number of reasons used "which are contrary to commonly known facts," and the number of reasons used which have no connection to the matter at hand (Taba and McGuire, 1942, 186). Lastly, the test seeks to determine whether students resolve issues by referencing democratic values or undemocratic values, by compromising, or by putting forward a rationalization.

Limitations of the Social Sensitivity Tests

When describing the Commission's measures of personal and social adjustment, I concluded that the tests failed to meet their stated objectives—they did not measure the adequacy of students' personal and social adjustment. In comparison, the tests of social sensitivity align better with their stated aim. In addition to measuring students' ability to apply social facts and generalizations to social problems, they directly assess students' values. Unlike the tests of adjustment, which fail to measure adjustment, these tests provide a measure of the degree to which students bring democratic commitments to their analysis of social issues. Nonetheless, the detail provided in the test result summary overstates the potential of this measurement strategy.

As the evaluators worked to design standardized tests, they applied their general definitions of "democratic" and "undemocratic" to particular policy directions. They defined democratic actions and reasons as those which defend "the interests of the general public or general welfare," and reflect commitments to "freedom of speech, equality of opportunity, and a decent standard of living, of rights of minorities and other underprivileged groups." Undemocratic reasons and actions emphasized efficiency and economic gain rather than human needs and values, they protect special privilege, and they support discriminatory procedures (Taba and McGuire, 1942, 183). The evaluators used these definitions to categorize particular policy options.

The static and inflexible nature of the distinctions they made, however, fails to capture the complexity and ambiguity inherent in deliberation of social issues. The structure of these tests implies that individuals committed to democracy would all recommend similar actions when faced with the same dilemmas. Clearly, this is not the case. Analysts who share a commitment to democratic values often reach different policy conclusions. Those with democratic values might share a commitment to freedom of speech, for example, but they could easily adopt different understandings of the implications of this commitment. Similarly, although analysts committed to democracy often might argue that government should regulate industry, in numerous cases many analysts with a democratic orientation would not support government regulation. Those who designed this exam rule out this possibility. Their approach also fails to offer guidance in cases where two or more "democratic" values conflict.

Not only are the test designers inattentive to these complexities, they also, and without explanation, basically define democratic behavior or values as those which coincide with liberal and socialist political ideology. The statement, "Since employers have to bear the expense of making improvements in working conditions, they should have a voice in deciding what changes should be made" is labeled "undemocratic" (Taba and McGuire, 1942, 181). Why? One could easily argue that all parties affected by a decision should have a voice in the decision process.

My point here is not simply that those designing these tests should have adopted more objective categorization schemes. I also want to question the notion that objective assessments of specific policies as "democratic" or "undemocratic" can be made. Once important and complex questions are raised, distinctions between democratic and undemocratic values blur. There is not a single "democratic" answer to a given problematic situation. As they worked to specify democratic and undemocratic values, those who designed these tests neglected the complexity of the goal they pursued. Rather than emphasizing the importance of informed debate and experimentation in the practice of democracy, they defined "democracy" in accordance with a liberal political ideology and they implied that a democratic orientation has specifiable policy implications.[6]

Strengths of the Social Sensitivity Tests

Despite these problems, the test described above and the others that accompanied it clearly represent a dramatic departure from mainstream testing practices and a thoughtful first step toward assessment of the Commission's ambitious goal. These tests measured more than students' knowledge of economics, history, or politics. They also assessed students' ability to apply such understandings in varied contexts, and they recorded the value orientation students used when responding to particular social problems.

As a result, these tests could be used in a variety of ways. If given by a teacher at the beginning of a year, the tests could be used "to *diagnose the strengths and weaknesses of the individuals in his class*" (Taba and McGuire, 1942, 240, emphasis in original). Did students use economic generalizations with accuracy? Were they frequently swayed by slogans rather than by logical arguments? Did students use a consistent set of values to guide their conclusions?

If given toward the end of a year or after a unit that focused students' attention on these concerns, the tests could also help a teacher *"check the effectiveness of his curriculum"* (240, emphasis in original). Could students employ social facts and generalizations with accuracy when considering responses to particular social problems? Were the values implicit in their reasoning consistent or did they vary with the topic? As noted earlier, much of the curricular change pushed by participating schools aimed to promote "social sensitivity." These tests could be used to assess whether "first-hand exploration of the community and use of literary material to illustrate social problems [or] democratic processes in administering school affairs [developed] personal democratic attitudes" (Taba and McGuire, 1942, 241).[7]

Reliability and Validity

Whether assessing measures of personal and social adjustment or social sensitivity, the evaluation team was committed to maintaining the same kinds of standards used to assess measures of mainstream goals:

> The usefulness of this instrument, as of any instrument, is determined by (1) how adequately it measures what it sets out to measure [validity] and (2) how reliable a particular set of the students' responses is likely to be. (Taba and McGuire, 1942, 190)

The evaluation team paid considerable attention to these concerns. For example, when assessing the tests of social sensitivity, they tested the consistency of students' scores with the students' behavior (as reported by teachers). They also transcribed detailed interviews with 45 students, which focused on the same issues the tests aimed to measure. A panel of four judges then considered whether the answers students provided during these lengthy interviews corresponded to the answers students provided on the exams. In addition, the evaluators carefully judged whether the impressions left by the particular method of scoring and summarizing test results adequately conveyed the findings of the particular exams. Finally, they checked to make sure that their exams measured students' values and ability to apply social facts and generalizations, and were not simply measures of "general intelligence." They also had students take the American Council Psychological Examination to see whether the measure of intelligence provided by this test correlated with scores students received on the test of social sensitivity. After extensive study and some revision of exams based on the results, the Commission concluded that "this test has sufficient validity and reliability to be a useful instrument for diagnosis" (Taba and McGuire, 1942, 197).

Comment: Overall Value of Having Designed Quantitative Measures

While recognizing the weaknesses of these attempts to evaluate the achievement of alternative priorities, it is important to emphasize both that this was the first cut at a very ambitious goal and that it accomplished much of value. First, in a variety of ways the tests created by the Commission demonstrate that policy analysts can collect a great deal of data that can help both educators and analysts consider students' progress toward humanistic and democratic goals. A second very important benefit of this process was the process itself. The Commission designed these tests in full consultation with educators in the participating schools. As the teachers helped to construct these exams and were trained to interpret the results, they simultaneously were led to further their own understanding of these complex issues and of their possible implications for the educational process.

DID THE PROGRESSIVELY EDUCATED STUDENTS SUCCEED IN COLLEGE?

In September 1936 the first graduates from the 30 schools were admitted to college. They had not completed the traditional unit requirements and had instead received a diverse array of educational experiences.

> What would become of these young guinea pigs? . . . Would they more or less en masse augment the gruesome list of flunk-outs? Would they turn out to be college loafers? Or dilettanti? Or possibly greasy grinds? Or obnoxious bolsheviks? Or . . . just regular college students? (McConn, 1942, xx)

To test the impact of these progressive approaches, 1,475 students from participating schools "were matched on the basis of sex, age, race, scholastic aptitude scores, home and community background, interests, and probable future" (Aiken, 1942a, 109) with similar students who had prepared in traditional ways for college. These students were interviewed periodically throughout their college careers, and records of their grades, academic honors, and extracurricular activities were kept.

A great deal was riding on this evaluation. As Aiken (1942a) explains, some proponents viewed the study as "an unnecessary and dangerous innovation," and some critics were pleased that "Progressive Education now had enough rope to hang itself" (23–24). The results were "a bit of an anticlimax for everybody concerned" (McConn, 1942, xx). When all was said and done, the evaluators concluded that the effect of students' high school program on their college success was minimal:

> These graduates of progressive schools have not set the colleges on fire, as some progressives may have hoped they would. On the other hand, they ... came out a little ahead of a comparison group. (McConn, 1942, xx–xxi)

Where differences existed, they were small. Still, on numerous valued outcomes, it was the students from the progressive programs that outperformed the others—if only slightly. When compared with similar students from traditional high schools, students from participating schools "earned a slightly higher total grade average, ... received slightly more academic honors in each year," and were slightly more likely to participate in artistic, theatrical, and musical extracurricular activities (Chamberlin et al., 1942, 207). Their grades in foreign languages and their rates of participation in religious groups, social service activities, and organized sports were all slightly lower. These differences were all very small, generally between 1 and 4 percentage points. The first-year students from progressive high schools, for example, had college grade point averages of 2.44, while the grades of similar students from traditional high schools averaged 2.40 (Chamberlin et al., 1942, 27).

The most convincing evidence that progressive schools were more "effective" came from comparisons of the success of students from the six most experimental schools with that of the students from the six least experimental schools. Researchers found that "the graduates of the most experimental schools were strikingly more successful than their matches," while "there were no large or consistent differences between the least experimental graduates and their comparison group" (Aiken, 1942b, 142–43).[8]

REACTIONS OF MAINSTREAM ANALYSTS AND EDUCATORS

The Eight-Year Study was designed to do much more than change and evaluate 30 progressive schools. The Commission also hoped to provide the models and convincing evidence needed to spread progressive approaches to secondary education throughout the country. It did not accomplish this goal.

The preface to the Commission's fourth volume had noted that the impact of progressive education on college performance was no longer the central concern of the educators who ran the Eight-Year Study: "[T]he problem of mastering and using [progressive approaches] turned out to be so difficult, complex, and engrossing that the original problem of college entrance requirements was almost lost sight of and forgotten" (McConn, 1942, xviii). But if this concern was of secondary importance to members of the Commission, it remained the prime concern of both the public and of mainstream analysts and educators. Whether in newspapers, popular magazines, or academic journals, commentaries on the Eight-Year Study focused on the performance of participating students in college and on the implications of this study for college entrance requirements. Benjamin Fine (1942), for example, wrote a lengthy article in the *New York Times* on the study. He briefly mentioned that the Commission recommended that "secondary schools re-evaluate their curricula and discard many of the artificial barriers that now separate various subject areas" (5). However, other than this and two other similarly vague sentences describing the curricular changes associated with the study, the entire article focused on these students' performance in college and on the desirability of particular college entrance requirements. Similarly, debates surrounding the study's value, which appeared in journals for educators, generally included a few references to the alternative curricula of the participating schools and then provided extensive detail on the findings regarding the students' performance in college (see, for example, Lancelot, 1943, 1945; Tyler, 1944; Johnson, 1946, 1950, 1951; Diederich, 1951).

It is often easiest to tell what people care about by looking at what they choose to contest. When criticizing the study, analysts focused almost exclusively on the inadequacy of the comparisons made between the college performance of study participants and nonparticipants. Both the critics and those who defended the study from these attacks, took mainstream measures of academic success as unproblematic proxies for desirable outcomes.

This surprised me. I had expected the Commission's alternative agenda to be met with critiques on many levels. Should schools really focus on democracy as a way of life? Were the measures proposed for student interests and social sensitivity reasonable? Does teacher/pupil planning undermine teachers' authority or the ability to focus students' attention in productive ways?

As it turned out, these issues generally were ignored by those who criticized the study. The critiques of the evaluation of the Eight-Year Study focused on the Commission's method of assessing student achievement of mainstream goals in college.

W. H. Lancelot (1943) initiated debate on the Eight-Year Study with a front-page article in the journal *School and Society*. Although he agreed that students from the progressive schools slightly outperformed those with whom they were paired, he questioned the conclusion that these differences can be attributed to progressive techniques. Instead, he argued that students in the participating schools were more successful because they had attended better funded schools. This money attracted more talented teachers and made it possible to have smaller classes.[9]

Several months later, Ralph Tyler (1944) responded. He said that careful analysis of the data revealed that the participating schools were not better funded than their counterparts and did not have smaller classes.

Lancelot (1945) was not convinced. He criticized the study's authors for not making their data available to the public and stated that his own estimates did not align with the data Tyler presented. Moreover, he complained that

> the voice of the advocate rings out so shrill and clear—and so often—throughout the report that attitudes of weariness and even of resistance are set up in the minds of thoughtful open-minded readers. (282)

Though aggressive, this exchange was more respectful than much of the dialogue between progressives and their critics. Some who criticized the Eight-Year Study could hardly contain their contempt for progressive education. Helmer G. Johnson (1950) labeled the Eight-Year Study "nothing but a hoax and a fraud" (339). In a series of articles (1946, 1950, 1951) he outlined methodological problems caused by selection bias, regression to the mean, and the Commission's use of aptitude test scores. He presented evidence indicating that the matched pairs of students might have been created in ways that made it likely that students from participating schools were slightly more talented than those with whom they were matched.

Johnson's analysis does not justify his conclusion that "the procedure used in the Eight-year Study . . . marks a new low in the quality of present-day educational research" (1951, 42). Accompanying his systematic discussion of methodological issues are numerous statements that demonstrate his contempt for progressive practices:

> If we must have such things as ineffective, disorderly Progressive education, the writer suggests that it be limited to the lowest 25 percent in intelligence where it will do little harm and that the rest of the pupils be given the opportunity to benefit from a stimulating, practical, well-balanced standard curriculum. (1950, 339)

The tone and target of these exchanges tell us as much as their substance. Those who attacked the Eight-Year Study never carefully engaged the Commission's alternative priorities. They focused on the part of the study that was probably the least methodologically vulnerable. Instead of offering a systematic critique of the Commission's ability to assess students' democratic character or their personal and social adjustment, critics of the study sought to undermine the evidence on college success. They adopted this focus even though the differences noted in the study were very small (Chauncey, 1941, was an exception). Perhaps of equal importance, those who defended the study never challenged their critics' exclusive focus on traditional concerns. Rather than arguing that judgments regarding the success of their project demanded attention to more than the impact of their schools on students' academic performance in college, they argued that their measures of this performance were accurate.

LOOKING BACK ON THE EIGHT-YEAR STUDY

In many respects, the Eight-Year Study was remarkable. It fostered dozens of innovative educational approaches that both students and teachers found rewarding. In the process, the project broke new and important ground by demonstrating the feasibility and desirability of such practices as site-based management, teacher/pupil planning, and teacher development workshops. In addition, original approaches to evaluation and documentation also were developed. As Ralph Tyler (1980) reminds us, the Eight-Year Study represented the first large-scale effort to appraise schools by analyzing "questionnaires, observations, and samples of products, as well as tests" (32). Finally, and perhaps most important, this study provides reformers with the first step toward a still unrealized goal. Those committed to democratic education can learn much from the study's accomplishments, from the barriers that limited success, and from the spirit that energized the movement. As Kathy Irwin (1991) writes in *Progressive Education for the 1990s:*

> For those of us committed to the democratic tradition of struggle, the Eight-year Study is both our ancestor and friend, reminding us that the idea and broad practice of democracy must remain the center-piece of our lives as citizens, teachers, and students. (59)

CONCLUSIONS

Though an important event for numerous reasons, the Eight-Year Study failed to accomplish its primary goal. It failed to bring progressive educational practices to the nation's high schools. It also failed to change the form and focus of policy deliberations. Neither the media nor the educational community paid extensive attention to this study. The book summarizing the study sold only 6,400 copies, and the volume documenting the changes that took place in each of the 30 schools sold fewer than 1,000 copies. When a group of participants gathered in 1950, 8 years after the end of the study, they concluded that "the evaluation program introduced by the Eight-year Study had been forgotten" and that "college entrance requirements had been tightened with too few admission officers aware of the results of the study" (Redefer, 1950, 34).

The most profound signal of the study's limited ability to transform practice comes from Frederick Redefer. Redefer had been the director of the Progressive Education Association when the study took place. In 1950 he surveyed the participating schools and found that only "two of the fifteen schools reporting attested that some of the 'spirit' of the Eight-year Study remained" (35). As one headmaster put it, "The strong breeze of the Eight-year Study has passed and now we are getting back to fundamentals" (35). The significance of this finding was not lost on critics of progressive practices. As Johnson (1951) pointed out, "If the 30 schools themselves are abandoning the experimental methods developed in the Eight-year Study, why should other schools adopt them?" (42).

How might one explain this outcome? The scale of this experiment, the status of those involved, and the generally positive findings were not enough to bring change. Why? Many attribute this result to the war (see Cremin, 1961; Aiken, 1953). The study ended in 1942, the explanation goes, and attention was focused elsewhere.

In many respects, this explanation is surely correct—but a broader explanation is needed as well. While it was clearly difficult to argue for experimental educational reform in the popular press in the midst of World War II, educators certainly could have paid greater attention to this study. College admissions officers could have altered their practices. At the very least, the participating schools could have maintained their experimental programs. With the end of the war, many practices resumed that had been placed on hold. The war in and of itself is not sufficient to explain the modest impact of the Eight-Year Study.

Another contributing, and perhaps more fundamental, factor responsible for the difficulties faced by proponents of the Eight-Year Study concerns the culture of mainstream policy analysis. I believe that one central lesson of the Eight-Year Study is that the norms, values, and technologies embedded in the culture of mainstream policy analysis are poorly suited to record, report, and promote the desirable aspects of progressive educational efforts.

First, the values and priorities of mainstream policy analysts differ dramatically from those of progressive educators. As a result of these values, many benefits of progressive practices receive little attention from policy analysts. I am referring not only to critics like Helmer Johnson who believe that progressive techniques reject the most sacred traditional educational values. Many analysts and much public sentiment is more charitable. However, while many are relatively tolerant of these alternative approaches, their analysis rarely focuses on progressive goals. Consequently, mainstream analysts were not particularly concerned with either the alternative assessment strategies developed by the Commission or the results of these new tests. They focused on the academic college performance of the study's participants (Lancelot, 1943, 1945; Tyler, 1944; Johnson, 1946, 1950, 1951; Diederich, 1951). For those running the Eight-Year Study, in contrast, ensuring college performance was a constraint—not the ultimate goal (Aiken, 1942a).

Second, just as the goals of mainstream analysts often align poorly with those of progressive educators, the means of assessing—the conventions and technologies of policy analysis—are often inappropriate for evaluating the attainment of progressive priorities. As became apparent during the discussion of the Commission's effort to assess students' social sensitivity, standardized, objective, and decontextualized measures can take analysts only so far. Educators understood democratic processes to emphasize informed public deliberation, concern for fellow citizens, and the development of individual priorities and interests that reflect the needs of the community. Concern for reliability and validity can help in the design of useful measures, but the value of these "scientific" criteria for assessments of "democratic character" is ultimately constrained by the subjective and context-dependent nature of democratic behavior. The objective standards that mainstream policy analysts seek generally cannot consider all that is relevant. There is a tension between the creation of precise numeric measures of democratic character and the creation of meaningful measures.

Third, findings on these matters are also very difficult to report. Mainstream analysts currently lack the language and set of conceptual categories needed to succinctly articulate student progress with respect to these democratic goals. The charts describing student performance (see, for example, Smith and Tyler, 1942, p. 185) succeed in providing some useful information about a given student's values and knowledge base; however, the complex nature of the format would make using these data to evaluate macro-level policy concerns quite difficult.

Fourth, the culture of mainstream policy analysis also reflects the preferences of those who work in bureaucracies (Majone, 1989). These clients of policy analysts want clearly specified goals and means to promote those goals. A progressive educational orientation, however, is often at odds with this desire. Indeed, progressive methods of evaluation and policy analysis, by making their subjective nature explicit and by asking teachers to make context-dependent judgments, threaten bureaucrats and policy analysts whose claim to legitimacy is rooted in their scientific approach. Moreover, these methods and the values they reflect will often conflict with analysts' desire to make standardized comparisons and issue bureaucratic mandates (see Swidler, 1982). Progressive priorities regarding individual development and the promotion of democratic social relations, for example, are often best approached indirectly. Bureaucracies can mandate that students receive lessons on human decency or on the value of free and full discussions among community members, but these and other goals are better approached through a process Dewey ([1938] 1963, 48) labels collateral learning. They are achieved indirectly, through students' experiences studying other issues and through other experiences both in and out of school.

Much of the motivation behind teacher/pupil planning and the cooperative experience-based curriculum, as described earlier, reflected these progressive ideals. Such approaches require that teachers make judgments that reflect the particular setting as well as students' interests and needs. As a result, this curriculum cannot be mass produced. In addition, processes such as teacher/pupil planning and experience-based curriculum lead to outcomes that often cannot be

specified in advance. This places policy analysts, evaluators, and bureaucrats in a difficult, or at least new, position. They must find ways
to design and assess programs without granting primacy to a predetermined set of goals or methods, so as to secure space for practitioners'
professional judgment on these matters.[10]

Thus, a variety of cultural commitments make it difficult for policy
analysts and evaluators to market this orientation, and many technical
constraints remain even after outside commitment to these goals has
been secured. While recognition of these barriers is important, it is
also important for analysts to remember that support for this elusive
goal is firmly rooted in our culture. As Franklin D. Roosevelt wrote
in 1939:

> Education for democracy cannot merely be taken for granted. What
> goes on in the schools every hour of the day, on the playground and
> in the classroom, whether reflecting methods of control by the
> teacher, or opportunities for self-expression by pupils, must be
> checked against the fact that children are growing up to live in a de-
> mocracy. That the schools make worthy citizens is the most important
> responsibility placed upon them. (in Carnegie Foundation for the Ad-
> vancement of Teaching, 1992, 85)

Joseph Featherstone (1991) reminds us that "progressive" educators are often ignorant of their own history. Living in what he calls the
"United States of Amnesia," these educators continually struggle to
develop clear conceptions of their goals, appropriate educational practices, and strategies to promote their alternative agenda (ix). The Eight-
Year Study provides a place from which others might begin. It also
offers a sense of the obstacles reformers may encounter on the journey.

8
Conclusion: Reframing Educational Policy

Currently, the vast bulk of mainstream policy analysis reflects utilitarian and rights-oriented commitments to utility, equality, and efficiency. This orientation does not rule out interest in other concerns. Those committed to individual liberty, for example, still may value utility and supportive, if voluntary, communities. Similarly, utilitarians often will support proponents of justice and fulfillment of personal potential because these concerns frequently further their primary goal.

Nonetheless, as I have argued in previous chapters, one's ethical orientation is consequential. Each perspective implies distinct agendas, methods of assessment, and ways of choosing sides when conflicts arise. At times these differences result in questions of emphasis. Utilitarians and rights theorists, for example, both might want higher academic standards instituted through state-level curriculum frameworks. The utilitarians might emphasize the importance of tying these frameworks to learning goals that will increase students' economic productivity. Rights theorists, in contrast, might be concerned primarily that teachers in underfunded districts be given the staff development they need to adapt to this new set of state requirements.

Differing priorities also can lead to direct conflicts over policy goals. Humanists might object, for example, to the emphasis other groups place on academic learning. Rights theorists might complain that democratic communitarian commitments threaten individual liberty.

In short, utilitarians, communitarians, rights theorists, humanists, and others bring markedly different concerns to the design, implementation, and assessment of educational policies. To the extent that utilitarian and rights-oriented perspectives dominate policy analysis, other important concerns often are obscured or neglected.

When making the case that analysts should consider a broader range of ethical priorities, I decided to focus on democratic communitarian and humanistic perspectives. These social and psychological theories provide compelling visions of individual and social development and harbor significant implications for educational practice. Despite their value as frames for policy discussions, they do not receive systematic attention from analysts and evaluators.[1] How, then, and when should analysts committed to broadening the focus of policy discussions pursue this goal?

CONTEXTUAL CONSIDERATIONS—POLITICAL PRESSURES AND TECHNICAL LIMITATIONS

For the most part, analysts who hope to enlarge the range of priorities that inform policy deliberations would not apply a particular set of principles to all policy situations. Policy analysts and evaluators are subject to numerous political pressures and technical limitations. These constrain their ability to pursue nonmainstream priorities. In this respect their task differs from that of political theorists whose more abstract analysis often is freed from numerous contextual complexities and empirical uncertainties. When selecting opportunities to push for alternatives, policy analysts consider what is technically and politically possible. As Aaron Wildavsky (1987) explains, policy analysts accept "the democratic institutions in which they find themselves, basing change both upon popular consent and elite understanding, each of which is in short supply" (xxxii).

Analysts generally try to be sensitive to the norms of their profession, the political legitimacy of their goals and methods, and the feasibility of their proposals. Do data support their position? Does the public value their goal? Can powerful interest groups block or redirect their efforts? Do practitioners have the knowledge and resources needed to bring about the desired result? These are questions they ask.

When marketing their alternative agendas, analysts also must consider their audience. There is probably more space for discussion of humanistic concerns in an evaluation of Head Start prepared for a school board, for example, than in one prepared for a congressional committee. In addition, analysts must attend to the programmatic barriers they face and set reasonable expectations. The kinds of experience-based curriculum described in Chapter 7, for instance, may appeal to educators hoping to promote democratic communities in schools, but designing and implementing such curriculum takes time and training as well as financial and organizational support. Since proponents of democratic communities and experience-based education rarely will be able to provide optimal conditions for promoting these reforms, issues of feasibility need to be considered.

The relevance of a humanistic or a democratic communitarian lens also will vary depending on the issue being assessed. When evaluating the trade-offs associated with Chubb and Moe's school choice proposal, for example, democratic communitarian concerns may be particularly relevant. Analysts can appeal to long-held public commitments to democratic control. In his discussion of school choice, Ernest Boyer (1992) reminds us:

> From the very first, this nation has committed itself to community-based education, with citizens in each neighborhood coming together to support the education of children. (xvii)

Democratic communitarian priorities may be less relevant for discussions of school finance. Mainstream sentiments regarding school spending are tied closely to utilitarian assessments of the return on public investments in human capital and to matters of equity. Similarly, humanistic perspectives probably offer more insights into debates on curriculum than into discussions of school governance structures.

In short, though marginal to most policy discussions, these alternative perspectives resonate with some strongly held cultural commitments. Analysts can broaden the focus of policy deliberations by highlighting the neglect of these concerns. Those interested in pursuing this agenda, however, also must identify and respond strategically to the constraints imposed by long-established norms, political pressures, and limits on resources and know-how. As the Progressive Education Association's experience with the Eight-Year study demonstrates, these norms, political pressures, and technical limitations are often formidable obstacles.

This is not to say that analysts should passively accept these constraints. Analysts' work is shaped by their environment, but it is an environment they also help to shape. While they must be sensitive to and think strategically about the limits they face, those hoping to promote alternatives also must work to create a policy climate receptive to the kinds of changes they value. What might that mean?

CHANGING NORMS AND CAPACITIES WHILE CREATING POLITICAL SUPPORT FOR ALTERNATIVES

Those working to shift the orientation of mainstream policy analysis must, as a first step, demonstrate the need to ask fundamental questions regarding the purpose of schools and their connection to the broader society. As shown in earlier chapters, the rhetorical commitments to notions of democracy and human potential found in policy documents are generally superficial. These phrases are invoked because of the importance they hold in our culture, but little careful attention is paid to their meaning or to the implications of these ethical orientations.

Moreover, when used in policy discussions, the understandings applied to these terms often embody fundamental commitments to utility and individual rights. Analysts argue that democracy demands a rights-oriented commitment to equality of opportunity. They do not methodically consider the implications of a Deweyan commitment to democracy as a form of communal life. Similarly, analysts proclaim that "the poor school [academic] performance of many students signals untapped human potential." The number of students who score above grade level on a test in reading is routinely assessed. The number who find that reading enriches their lives is not. Subtle aspects of a child's affective development often receive little or no systematic attention.

Of central importance, then, for those interested in creating a climate receptive to alternatives, is the need to document both the extent of this neglect and its cost. While recognizing the importance of utilitarian and rights-oriented commitments to equity and excellence, those hoping to bring changes must argue that, on their own, these frameworks are often inadequate. To be effective, it seems likely that this case must be made through examples as well as through theoretical arguments. I chose to apply these alternative perspectives to specific issues of policy and practice, hoping to specify ways in which focusing on alternative perspectives could enrich policy dialogues. In addition to providing analysis driven by these concerns, it also would be helpful to provide examples of schools that explicitly emphasize these priorities.

ENABLING ASSESSMENT OF ALTERNATIVE PRIORITIES

To the extent that the case for assessing alternative priorities gains credibility, a related need becomes even clearer. Analysts must do more than demonstrate the importance of attending to nonmainstream goals; they also must develop assessment strategies that reflect the goals and logics of these alternative social doctrines.

Currently, educational policy analysts concerned with utilitarian and rights-oriented perspectives can draw from a vast empirical and theoretical literature. A great deal of applied and conceptual work in the economics, sociology, and psychology of education relates directly to these goals. In addition, a great deal of empirical data pertaining to these concerns have been and continue to be collected. Much less information is available for educational policy analysts committed to democratic communitarian or humanistic goals. These analysts lack both clear conceptions of their priorities and ways to monitor their performance.

The approaches developed during the Eight-Year Study to assess these alternative concerns, though flawed, were an extraordinary first step. Equally remarkable, and perhaps a cause for alarm, is the fact that 50 years later little has been done to build on these efforts. Those hoping to promote policy analysis consistent with democratic communitarian and humanistic goals must demonstrate that they can deliver meaningful commentaries, informed by their alternative concerns.

CHANGING THE FORM AS WELL AS THE FOCUS OF POLICY ANALYSIS

Clearly, analysts' focus would shift if they began to assess the achievement of humanistic or democratic communitarian goals. In addition to monitoring the achievement of academic goals, they would attend to patterns of social interaction, for example, and to students' psychological health. As one begins to consider various methods for assessing these concerns, it also becomes clear that this shift in focus may imply a fundamental shift in the form of policy analysis as well.

Currently, mainstream analysts strive for "scientific" and "objective" assessments of policies and their effects by measuring proxies for utility and equality. This approach, with its emphasis on standardized measures of success and failure, will be difficult to maintain if mainstream concerns for academic achievement and the attainment of credentials are replaced by democratic communitarian and humanistic concerns for the "healthy" development of individuals and communities. Those committed to these alternative perspectives reject the mainstream emphasis on predetermined goals and standards (high test scores, low dropout rates, equal spending). Analysts driven by democratic communitarian and humanistic goals and logic understand the relative desirability of a particular outcome to be closely tied to the particular context. One must know a great deal about a student, for example, before the desirability of his or her development or growth can be assessed. Similarly, no fixed set of criteria can be used to judge the desirability of the community that exists at a school or in a classroom. Democracy is a process, but not a prespecified set of procedures.

Thus, neither democratic communitarian nor humanistic concerns will fit easily into mainstream forms of policy analysis for which "scientific" assessments of standardized inputs, outputs, and processes represent the bottom line. Analysts will need to develop ways to interpret outcomes and processes that are informed by these alternative theories and by an understanding of the specific context.

To summarize, a number of tasks face those hoping to create an environment in which policy analysts' work embodies commitments to either democratic communitarian or humanistic ethical systems; they must build greater support for their alternative perspectives; they must further conceptualize the implications of these perspectives for educational policy; they must develop methods of assessment that reflect these priorities; and they must make the case that these less scientifically based discussions of policy analysis are legitimate. Clearly, this is a tall order. It requires advances in assessment and staff development in addition to changing the norms of the culture in which analysts work.

Despite these difficulties, it is a challenge worth pursuing. Many parents, teachers, administrators, and school board members are already committed to democratic communitarian and humanistic goals. Methods of assessment and analytic frameworks that reflect such alternative priorities can provide these educators with incentives and direction. Mainstream priorities, in contrast, often present reformers committed to this kind of change with barriers and diversions.

In addition, this alternative form of policy analysis can deliver guidance and support to those working on a variety of current reform initiatives. School-based management, cooperative learning, multicultural curriculum, and curriculum attentive to multiple learning styles, for example, all have the potential to promote both democratic communitarian and humanistic goals.[2] The development of these reform movements will depend, in part, on the ways these initiatives are marketed and assessed. Approaches to cooperative learning that strive to improve individual students' scores on math tests may be quite different from those that aim to promote a sense of democratic community. Similarly, it matters whether school-based management is viewed as a way to help educators respond to the broadly conceived needs and interests of students, whether this enterprise is judged by its impact on reading scores, or whether the democratic nature of school-based management receives the primary attention of evaluators. Alternative approaches to policy analysis could therefore be very important tools.

They could be used to assess and to help shape the form and focus of these and other reform efforts.

Finally, these alternative frameworks can promote consideration of matters that might otherwise be passed over. Currently, calls for a national curriculum and national tests—long anathema to our country's commitment to local control—receive unprecedented attention. But what goals get considered? On which concerns will these goals and tests focus?

Increasingly, educators argue for systemic reform. By designing state-level curriculum frameworks, for example, they hope to coordinate the actions of educators and policy makers on different levels so that all can focus on common goals. Which goals? Whose goals? And why?

If one were to ask business leaders, teachers, principals, school board members, parents, and students how schools can foster the development of both individuals and society, one would hear a variety of answers. Policy analysts may well share this broad array of concerns, but they devote systematic attention primarily to equity, efficiency, and excellence.

Equity, efficiency, and excellence are important. However, to use Maslow's quip, when critiquing behaviorist psychology, "When your thing is swinging a hammer, everything starts looking like a nail." Schools can promote a variety of individual and social goals. When analysts neglect these alternatives, the costs are substantial.

Summary of the Four Perspectives

1. MAINSTREAM UTILITARIANISM

Social policy goals. Utilitarians hope to promote aggregate utility—the greatest good for the greatest number.

Goals applied to education. Utilitarian educators focus on the ways education can promote individual happiness and social welfare. They emphasize the value of human capital development for both individuals (private good) and society (public good). They link education to progress and increases in productivity.

Rhetoric consistent with these goals. "A nation at risk," "education as the key to competition with Japan," "If you think education is expensive, try ignorance," "productive citizens," "human capital."

Analytic logic. Utilitarians identify a proxy for utility, operationalize it, monitor it, and maximize it. They compare costs and benefits, assume that individuals are rational actors, and focus on efficiency. They believe that some individuals should sacrifice for the good of others if such an action raises total utility.

Logic applied to education. Educators who are utilitarians design curriculum and develop pedagogy so as to promote human capital. They align curriculum and pedagogy with the needs of the economy and they utilize production function and cost–benefit studies of educational outcomes (examples include the Coleman Report, cost–benefit studies on Head Start, studies of the impact of computers and class size on learning, etc.).

Rhetoric consistent with this logic. "Aligning the curriculum with the needs of society," "cost-effective policies," "vocational education."

2. THREE VISIONS OF RIGHTS

A System of Natural Liberty—A Libertarian Perspective

Social policy goals. Libertarians believe that careers should be open to talents. They generally wish to promote a free market system in which individuals (or, perhaps in the case of children, individuals' parents) experience complete liberty as long as their actions do not infringe on the rights (e.g., property) or liberties of others.

Goals applied to education. Libertarians argue either that education should be used to help children mature into adults who can then pursue their own personal goals or that education should be guided by the desires of students (or, more commonly, their parents) so long as those desires do not infringe on the rights or liberties of others.

Rhetoric consistent with these goals. "Free to choose," "competition," "Darwinian selection," "education for freedom," "self-made man."

Analytic logic. Libertarians adhere to the logic of the market. They seek to create a free market and judge as just any and all results of free and competitive processes. They object both to racial and gender barriers to access and to governmental policies that further the interests of particular groups.

Logic applied to education. Libertarian logic could be used to justify letting students be driven by their own intrinsic motivations, in which case schools would provide numerous options and let students (or parents) choose their course of study/action. Alternatively, libertarians might argue that students should focus on scholastic achievement in those areas that will maximize human capital and thereby future opportunities. Although libertarians might support the notion of publicly financed schools, they would prefer a voucher or choice system to a system run by the government (see Hayek, 1976, 84).

Rhetoric consistent with this logic. "Free market," "choice," "vote with your feet," "decentralize," "cut red tape," "teacher autonomy," "student autonomy," "electives," "pull yourself up by your bootstraps."

A System of Liberal Equality—A Meritocratic Perspective

Social policy goals. Liberal equality places emphasis on merit. (Merit is defined as the product of individual effort and ability.) The belief is that merit rather than economic, social, and cultural forces should determine outcomes. Rawls (1971) calls liberal equality the combination of fair equality of opportunity and efficiency. Those pursuing liberal equality want both legislation ensuring that careers are open to talented students, and they want compensatory strategies that enable all to develop talents and compete for desired goals and positions. Those following this goal make no attempt to compensate individuals for differences in natural assets, only for differences in social contingencies.

Goals applied to education. Meritocrats would be likely to argue that education should be equally available to all and that the rewards of education should be distributed on the basis of hard work and native ability. In addition, many meritocrats want an educational system that is structured to compensate those with fewer natural and/or social assets so that they will be prepared for a societal structure outside the schools that distributes goods on the basis of merit.

Rhetoric consistent with these goals. "Equality of opportunity," "meritocracy," "compensatory education," "need blind admissions."

Analytic logic. Meritocrats attempt to give all students equal opportunity and access to the opportunities available in society, and they support policies that try to decrease the advantages that accrue to some on the basis of race, class, gender, parental connections, and so on.

Logic applied to education. Meritocrats would attempt to create a level playing field in which all could compete for success in school. To the extent possible, they would attempt to equalize the distribution of the educational services individuals receive, and they would hope to find and attend to objective means of measuring performance. Meritocrats also would support compensatory programs aimed at neutralizing the barriers (e.g., poverty) to education that some encounter outside of school.

Rhetoric consistent with this logic. "Civil service exams," "compensatory education," "level playing field," "uniform curriculum," "Separate but equal is inherently unequal," "equity movement."

A System of Democratic Equality—A Rawlsian Perspective

Social policy goals. Democratic equality, the combination of fair equality of opportunity and the difference principle (Rawls, 1971, 75), calls meritocracy into question. Rawlsians do not believe individuals deserve their natural assets (DNA, physical strength) any more than they deserve the advantages they gain from social contingencies (familial support, race, class, gender). Policies consistent with this vision must take steps to maximize the interests of the least well off.

Goals applied to education. Those pursuing democratic equality might propose a variety of plans aimed at promoting fair equality of opportunity that align with the difference principle. They probably would hope to use education as a means of compensating for arbitrary distribution of social and natural goods, as a way of providing all students "equal" access to the tools they need to compete for the ends they value, and as a way of serving the interests of the least well off.

Rhetoric consistent with these goals. "Fair equality of opportunity,"

"Separate but equal is inherently unequal," "equity movement," "universal education," "equal outcomes."[1]

Analytic logic. Those pursuing democratic equality attempt to compensate for inequitable distribution of natural and/or social assets. They hope to arrange social institutions so as to maximize the well-being of the least well off.

Logic applied to education. Those pursuing democratic equality would attempt to compensate groups or individuals with unequal natural and/or social goods. These compensatory strategies might include Chapter I, Head Start, and mainstreaming. In addition, some attempts are made to promote equality of access to educational opportunity, anti-tracking, desegregation, and equality of school finance.

Rhetoric consistent with this logic. "Compensatory education," "equality of access," "Help those who are less fortunate," "Do unto others as you would have them do unto you."

3. DEMOCRATIC COMMUNITARIAN THOUGHT AND EDUCATIONAL POLICY ANALYSIS

Social policy goals. Democratic communitarians endorse Dewey's (1927) claim that "the clear consciousness of a communal life, in all its implications, constitutes the idea of democracy" (149). Members of such societies share a commitment to each other and are involved, at least in some sense, on a common project. They strive for a communal life, social harmony, shared interests, informed debate, and wholeness incorporating diversity. They seek to promote the support, sense of common mission, and sense of belonging that can come out of community, and to avoid the envy, alienation, destructive competition, and exploitation that can result from self-serving behavior of individuals.

Goals applied to education. Democratic communitarian educators aim to develop social attitudes and sensitivities. They want to create miniature communities and group projects in which students share interests, respect diversity, hold common goals, and take part in informed debates of important social issues.

Rhetoric consistent with these goals. "A nation at risk" (at least on the surface), "a community of scholars," "cooperative tasks," "community schools," "community school boards," "shared identity," "civic education," "wholeness incorporating diversity."

Analytic logic. Cooperative effort, support, and informed debate are valued. Two main criteria are used to assess the desirability of a given community: (1) "How numerous and varied are the interests which are consciously shared?" and (2) "How full and free is the interplay with other forms of association?" (Dewey, [1916] 1966, 83).

Logic applied to education. Democratic communitarians would focus on the educational process and consider the desirability of the miniature community created within the school or classroom. They would assess the impact of schools on students' character and on their abilities (both analytic and social) to further both individual and group goals.

Rhetoric consistent with this logic. "Group work," "cooperative learning," "collective identity," "shared interests," "include everyone," "How well did the class do?," "informed debate," "common core curriculum," "multicultural curriculum," "democratic education."

4. HUMANISTIC PSYCHOLOGY AND EDUCATIONAL POLICY ANALYSIS

Social policy goals. Psychological humanists advocate "the use and exploitation of talents, capacities, potentialities, etc. . . . reminding us of Nietzsche's exhortation, 'Become what thou art!'" (Maslow, 1954, 200–201). They seek to promote self-actualization, realization of potential, growth of the whole person, and exposure to a full range of life's experiences and emotions.

Goals applied to education. "To humanists, the goals of education are dynamic personal processes related to the ideals of personal growth, integrity and autonomy. Healthier attitudes toward self, peers, and learning are among their expectations. The ideal of self-actualization is at the heart of the humanistic curriculum. A person who exhibits this quality is not only coolly cognitive, but is also developed in aesthetic and moral ways . . . [the] self must be uncovered" (McNeil, 1985, 5).

Rhetoric consistent with these goals. "Self-actualization," "peak experiences," "self-understanding," "self-awareness," "child-centered school."

Analytic logic. Psychological humanists hope to free and empower individuals to direct their own growth. They believe that free individuals will embark on a course that is both natural and desirable. They strive to facilitate experiences that give rise to love, hate, anxiety, awe, mystery, and peak experiences. Such education is nondirective. Nonhierarchical settings are desirable.

Logic applied to education. Such educators ask: Can the schools meet students' diverse needs? Are students developing their full range of social, cognitive, and affective traits? Are there diverse offerings? Are the basic human needs of belonging, self-esteem, hunger, and safety being met? Is an open-ended, nonhierarchical setting being promoted through pupil–pupil interaction, less teacher authority, descriptive report cards, discovery learning, emphasis on student-directed learning, personal growth exercises, diverse offerings, varied goals, and means of assessing the educational experience?

Rhetoric consistent with this logic. "Student-directed learning," "educating the whole child," "teachers as facilitators," "nondirective," "intrinsic motivation," "education as therapy," "free schools."

Notes

CHAPTER 2

1. The words "maximize" and "minimize" were both created by Bentham (see Pitkin, 1990, 105).

2. I use the term "libertarian" to refer to those who promote the natural liberty perspective. I do not provide a detailed discussion of the system Rawls labels "natural aristocracy" because modern policy analysts appeal to this vision less frequently than they appeal to the others. Still, many do and have invoked this ideal, so it is worthy of attention. Natural aristocracy proponents believe in a combination of careers open to talents and the difference principle. Those who want social institutions guided by a natural aristocracy share libertarians' belief that careers should be open to talents, so they oppose discrimination based on personal prejudices against individual qualities that do not affect job performance (race, gender, looks, social class, family lineage, and the like). They also do not believe in government-sponsored compensation for those individuals born with fewer native assets. As a result, they believe, the most talented individuals will rise to positions of authority. This notion was central to Jefferson's support for popular education. He wanted to create a "natural aristocracy" based on virtue and talent, which he contrasted with an "artificial aristocracy," which reflected social class and family lineage. The difference between this perspective and the libertarian ideal is that the natural aristocracy was to be guided by the difference principle. That is, talented students would use their natural talents to promote the well-being of the less fortunate. Thus, educators might pay greater attention to gifted students, but there would be an expectation that these students would use their talents to better the interests of the poorer segments of the society (see Rawls, 1971, 74). For more on the grid, see ibid., 65.

3. Readers may note that Jefferson's vision is used to illustrate both the notion of a "natural aristocracy" and the notion of a meritocracy. The perspectives are different, but Jefferson's thinking spans both categories. To the extent that Jefferson's plan provided fair equality of opportunity through the provision of free public education, Jefferson is a meritocrat. James Giarelli and Rodman Webb (1980, 224), for example, place him in this category. However, to the extent that these schools fail to compensate students for unequal distribution of the social assets that promote school success, Jefferson's model fails to provide fair equality of opportunity. Instead it promotes a society in which careers are open to talents. This, combined with his belief that these talented leaders will serve the public interest and attend to the needs of the least well off makes Jefferson a proponent of a natural aristocracy.

The fact that one man's vision can align with categories that, from an analytic point of view, are so different is testimony to the complexity of "real world" policies and the limited ability of analytic models to cleanly capture these distinctions.

CHAPTER 3

1. It is worth noting that Plato also was a strong advocate of a natural aristocracy.

2. Even Rousseau's Émile was to be educated in isolation from corrupting society only so that he could meet his rational and ethical community responsibilities as an adult (see Oliver, 1982).

3. Throughout this book, I refer to John Dewey as a democratic communitarian. I do this despite his identification with liberalism. As his recent biographer writes, Dewey pursued "hybrid forms of liberal-communitarianism and democratic-socialism" (Westbrook, 1991, 550). I emphasize his democratic communitarian commitments because they are particularly relevant for discussions of educational policy and because they differ dramatically from mainstream policy goals that emphasize utility and individual rights.

In addition, although I use the word "communitarian," I do not mean to imply that Dewey's thought aligns with that of theorists such as MacIntyre and Etzioni, who also invoke this term. As I will demonstrate, Dewey's commitment to democracy shapes his communitarian sentiments.

4. The instrumental success of these schools, although not a main issue here, may be of interest to readers. Even though most of these schools operate without electricity or running water, with teachers who lack a high school diploma, with old textbooks, with no educational technology, and without any separation of students by age, grade, or ability, these students score at or above national norms on most standardized measures of achievement (Kachel, 1989).

5. Lawrence Kohlberg's Just Community Schools represent another attempt to blend Kantian notions of individual rights with communitarian commitments. In these schools students actively create functioning democratic communities that govern numerous aspects of these students' school experience. Kohlberg adopts the Just Community Schools approach because he feels it can facilitate transition through his sequence of moral development. Kohlberg's ultimate commitment, however, is to justice and not community (Power, Higgins, and Kohlberg, 1989).

6. See Gutmann (1982) for a discussion of the dilemmas facing utilitarians and rights theorists who strive to educate in a manner that remains neutral with respect to different ways of life.

7. Liberals need not accord students freedom to direct their own education. However, even when parents or educators direct students' education, those with liberal commitments have less latitude to direct the nature of individual growth than those who strive to foster democratic community.

8. Isaiah Berlin would later identify this as "negative freedom," meaning freedom from restraints.

CHAPTER 4

1. Rousseau's educational plan for women was substantially different.

2. It is important to note that even though Rousseau's pedagogic commitments share much with the orientation of humanistic psychologists, these humanists would not embrace his social theory. Rousseau's commitment to educating male children in isolation from social norms and constraints stemmed from his belief that this approach would foster their own "natural" rationality, which, in turn, would guide them as citizens once they reentered civil society. Indeed, it was this rationality that would help them identify and promote the general will, rather than their own narrow interests. For reasons outlined above, humanistic psychologists would be threatened by Rousseau's ideal of a general will.

CHAPTER 5

1. Some analysts emphasize the distinction between tracking and ability grouping. As Diane Ravitch (1985) explains, "Ability grouping permits students to take different amounts of time to reach roughly similar goals; tracking offers students vastly different kinds of educational programs [academic/ vocational/ general]" (278). In this chapter I will distinguish between these practices only when this distinction is needed to correctly interpret analysts' rhetoric.

2. One additional point is worth making. Both groups equated democracy with equality of opportunity not equality of result. The Committee of Ten wanted all students treated in similar ways. Advocates of tracking wanted students treated in equally appropriate ways. Neither group either anticipated or desired equal outcomes.

3. These layers include "the managing, leading, guiding class . . . skilled manual labor . . . the layer which is employed in buying, selling, and distributing. . . . Lastly, there is the thick fundamental layer engaged in household work, agriculture, mining, quarrying, and forest work" (218). These four layers "are indispensable, and, so far as we can see, eternal" (219).

4. See Eliot, [1905] 1961, 151.

5. In other writing Eliot seems less committed to such standardization. When addressing the National Education Association (NEA) in 1892 he wrote, "Every child is a unique personality. It follows, of course, that uniform programs and uniform methods of instruction, applied simultaneously to large numbers of children, must be unwise and injurious." (Eliot, [1892] 1961, 53–4).

6. Indeed, these educators generally emphasized a student's career as the

relevant feature of his or her life. Note Eliot's 1910 speech to the NEA, titled, "The Value During Education of the Life Career Motive." He stated that education "must be [modified] by the acceptance on the part of teachers and administrators of the functions of guiding children into appropriate life work" (in Preskill, 1989, 356).

7. President Clinton, then governor of Arkansas, was one of two cochairmen of this task force for the National Governors' Association and one of two elected officials on the 17 member Carnegie task force.

8. Numerous studies present similar data. Rosenbaum (1980) reports a study by Mason in which students said, for example, "I'm in the high group. . . . Kids in the other groups are retards," and "Kids in the bottom group don't care" (in Rosenbaum, 1980, 373).

9. The authors of the *Cardinal Principles of Secondary Education* expressed the belief that such organizations could bring unity to schools in which students were placed in different curricular tracks (Department of the Interior, [1918] 1928).

10. Many rights theorists would agree with this principle. In practice, however, educational policy analysts who stress justice and fairness also promote similar treatment.

11. The nature of these "core" experiences and "essential" skills would be decided through democratic deliberation at the school and school board level. Some guidelines might come from the state or national level. In addition, the perspectives of teachers and other educational professionals might inform the decision-making process.

CHAPTER 6

1. The High School and Beyond (HSB) survey is the largest comprehensive data set on American high school students.

2. There is a reference to Coleman's study *Equality of Educational Opportunity,* but, when discussing this report, Chubb and Moe do not address issues of educational equity.

3. In addition, some worry that students whose parents are alienated, already overburdened, or unable to gather and assess information on different schools will not be able to promote the best interests of their children (Wells, 1991). More generally, critics write that many of the regulations that may constrain efficiency are needed to protect students' rights. Glass and Matthews (1991) ask, "Have we reached an enlightened state in this country where those safeguards can be dispensed with for the sake of teachers' and administrators' autonomy?" (26).

4. In addition, at a time when resources are already in short supply, critics question the wisdom of asking the government to pay for the education of all the students who are currently in private schools (roughly 10 percent of the student population). Providing students with transportation and access to information, analysts charge, is also both difficult and expensive (ASCD, 1990; see

also Boyer, 1992). Finally, utilitarian concerns are voiced by critics who worry that choice proposals would lead to inefficiency, fraud, and/or bureaucratic regulatory agencies that would produce the same kind of constraints choice advocates want to avoid (see, for example, Shannon, 1990/1991).

5. My point is not that Gutmann is a communitarian. I am claiming only that her discussion includes communitarian concerns.

6. Despite their opposition to vouchers, neither Gutmann nor Walzer advocates the abolition of private schools entirely. As long as the percentage of students in these schools does not seriously undermine support for public schooling and as long as private schools do not significantly reinforce racial and class distinctions (neither worries about single-sex schools), they are comfortable supporting the rights of parents with strong preferences regarding the style, quality, or religious orientation of their children's education to select private schools (see Walzer, 1983, 219; Gutmann, 1987, 116–21).

7. This silence stands in stark contrast to the wide and substantially researched range of policy options put forward with respect to excellence and efficiency.

8. A recent and important exception is worth noting. Researchers studying reforms in Chicago have focused systematically on the qualities of school board deliberations. The Consortium on Chicago School Research, for example, examined the prevalence of differing kinds of local school politics. They placed schools in one of four categories depending on the political dynamics that characterized interactions between parents, teachers, administrators, and local school board members. They found that between 39% and 46% of the schools were characterized by "consolidated principal power." Both the school board and the teachers in these schools exercised little control. Between 4% and 9% of the schools had "adversarial politics." In these schools conflict between teachers, administrators, and school board members prevented meaningful progress toward school improvement. Between 14% and 24% of the schools were characterized by "maintenance politics." Here there was little conflict, but also little change. Finally, 23% to 32% of the schools were characterized by "strong democracy" (a term used by Benjamin Barber, 1984, to describe a Deweyan sense of democratic community). Teachers, parents, community members, and administrators in these schools engaged in meaningful and productive discussions about their goals and ways to attain them. While these categories and the method by which schools were judged might well be worthy of debate, this focus clearly reflects concern for democratic communitarian values (Bryk et al., 1993).

9. Traditional communitarians, of course, would not share this view. Educators committed to a particular tradition would not worry if school choice led to the development of schools that provided "less opportunity for personal change," since they would want schools that reinforced their particular conception of the good. They might well view the practice of creating ideologically homogeneous schools as both appropriate and desirable.

10. From a legal standpoint, parents probably would have ultimate control over these decisions. One would expect that a student's influence would

depend on his or her family as well as on his or her age. Though humanists would likely agree that parents should have a significant role in the decision process, especially for young children, they would want these decisions to reflect students' interests and developmental needs. Humanists would not want choices made by parents and students to reflect parental values, social norms, and careerist priorities. Empirical assessments of the values that guide these choices would be of tremendous interest to humanistic educators.

CHAPTER 7

1. Many of these schools had reputations for excellence. They included the Dalton Schools, Fieldston, Francis W. Parker, Germantown Friends, Horace Mann, Milton Academy, and New Trier Township High School.

2. The composition of the Commission may help to explain its emphasis on school-based change and the confidence it placed in teachers and administrators. Unlike many recent commissions, it had no representatives from business or industry, and no elected officials.

3. Generally, the programs developed in the private schools included all students.

4. The rhetoric used by educators in Tulsa and the other schools may imply a kind of commitment to equal treatment, but the practices of these schools will probably strike today's readers as grossly inadequate. Tulsa's schools, for example, were segregated. There were three public high schools for whites and a separate school for blacks (Thirty Schools, 1942, 643).

5. As Giles, McCutchen, and Zechiel (1942) point out, however, "Each pupil, of course, makes the decision as to what will be learned" (77).

6. These tests also highlight an issue that demonstrates some of the structural constraints on educators with progressive agendas. Some of the exams included questions about racial segregation and tracking systems. The answer key indicates that the "democratic" response was to support integration and heterogeneous grouping. Most of the schools these students attended, however, were racially segregated, and only students who were judged to have above-average ability participated in the study. This comment is not meant to belittle the efforts of these reformers. It is, however, extremely important to recognize how the work of reformers is often compromised by external social pressures.

7. It also should be pointed out that the Commission's assessments of democratic character focused on students' behavior (see Bulletin No. 1, *Anecdotal Records*, 1935). Attention to students' behavior was important for two related reasons. First, one gains a clearer sense of the way students analyze facts and make decisions when the decisions have real consequences. For example, a great deal could be learned by examining the way in which students responded to the plight of families facing poverty because of the Depression that could not be learned by reading students' abstract commentaries on poverty.

Second, if democracy is a way of life and if "the clear consciousness of a communal life, in all its implications, constitutes the idea of democracy" (Dewey, 1927, 149), then those assessing a school's impact on students' values need to assess the ways in which students interact while at school. Analysts interested in assessing the development of democratic character need to watch the ways in which students confront challenges. Do they work alone, do they compete, do they help one another?

Recognizing the need to study behavior, teachers at the 30 schools compiled anecdotal records. These records were designed to be used by individual teachers or by teams of teachers interested in reflecting on these concerns and on the impact of school organization and pedagogy on students' behavior. The records could also be used to monitor the behavior of individual students or classes over time.

8. Students from the most experimental schools had grade averages of 2.72, while their control group had averages of 2.60. In comparison, students from the least experimental schools had grade averages of 2.27, while their control group had averages of 2.28 (Chamberlin et al., 1942, 166). Similarly, only 21% of the students from the most experimental schools were judged "essentially selfish," as compared with 28% of the control group. Of the students from both the least experimental group and their control group, 41% were judged "essentially selfish" (Chamberlin et al., 1942, 169).

9. Though the bulk of the article focused on these mainstream issues, Lancelot (1943) included one paragraph in which he praised the pedagogic and curricular innovations promoted by the Commission. The "five-volume report of the study contains so many stimulating suggestions and ingenious solutions of vital educational problems," he wrote, "that we should be extremely tolerant toward its imperfections" (451).

10. This raises an additional issue as well. Bureaucrats are not the only ones who would be threatened by allowing teachers and students more freedom to make context-dependent judgments regarding curriculum in light of their own assessments of student and community needs. As Tyack (1974) and Callahan (1962) point out, those with political and economic power often use bureaucratic structures to advance their own agendas. While this observation does not negate the constraints imposed by various features of the culture of policy analysis, it does underscore the fact that this culture is only one of a number of factors that limit the spread of democratic education.

CHAPTER 8

1. These, of course, are not the only alternative social theories worthy of consideration. One might, for example, bring a Marxist perspective to policy analysis (see Bowles and Gintis, 1976) or one informed by an ethic of care (see Noddings, 1984, 1992a)—a variety of important and coherent perspectives exist. Value frameworks tied to cultural and religious outlooks might also be considered. Finally, the implications of other conceptions of democracy and human potential might be explored.

2. Though much of the motivation for these reforms draws on humanistic and democratic communitarian sensibilities, analysts generally, though not exclusively, rely on utilitarian and rights-oriented rationales when designing and assessing these efforts. In large part, I believe this stems from their lack of a framework with which to systematically consider many of their most prized goals.

APPENDIX

1. Note that the rhetoric surrounding democratic equality is similar to that surrounding meritocracy. Both systems share a commitment to providing fair equality of opportunity. Those endorsing democratic equality probably would be more committed to equal outcomes because of their commitment to the difference principle.

References

Adler, M. (1982). *The Paideia Proposal: An Educational Manifesto*. New York: Macmillan.

Aiken, W. (1942a). *Adventure in American Education*. Vol. 1, *The Story of the Eight-Year Study*. New York: Harper.

Aiken, W. (1942b). "An Adventure in American Education." *California Journal of Secondary Education* 17(3): 138–43.

Aiken, W. (1942c). Introduction to *Adventure in American Education*. Vol. 3, *Appraising and Recording Student Progress: Evaluation, Records and Reports in Thirty Schools*, edited by E. R. Smith and R. W. Tyler. New York: Harper.

Aiken, W. (1953). "The Eight-Year Study: If We Were to Do It Again." *Progressive Education* 31(1): 11–14.

Allan, S. (1991). "Ability-Grouping Research Reviews: What Do They Say About Grouping and the Gifted?" *Educational Leadership* 48(6): 60–65.

Association for Supervision and Curriculum Development (ASCD). (1990). *Public Schools of Choice*. Alexandria, VA: ASCD Issues Analysis.

Barber, B. R. (1984). *Strong Democracy: Participatory Politics for a New Age*. Berkeley: University of California Press.

Bastian, A. (1990). "School Choice: Unwrapping the Package." In *Choice in Education: Potential and Problems*, edited by W. L. Boyd and H. J. Walberg. Berkeley: McCutchan.

Becker, G. S. (1964). *Human Capital*. New York: Columbia University Press.

Bell, D. (1960). *The End of Ideology: On the Exhaustion of Political Ideas in the Fifties*. New York: Free Press.

Bell, L., and Schniedewind, N. (1989). "Realizing the Promise of Humanistic Education: A Reconstructed Pedagogy for Personal and Social Change." *Journal of Humanistic Psychology* 29(2): 200–223.

Bell, R. (1985). *The Culture of Policy Deliberations*. New Brunswick, NJ: Rutgers University Press.

Bellah, R.; Masden, R.; Sullivan, W.; Swidler, A.; and Tipton, S. (1985). *Habits of the Heart: Individualism and Commitment in American Life*. New York: Harper & Row.

Benson, C. S. (1991). "Definition of Equity in School Finance in Texas, New Jersey, and Kentucky." *Harvard Journal on Legislation* 28 (395): 401–21.

Bentham, J. (1843). "Principles of Penal Law." In *Works of Jeremy Bentham*, Vol. 1. Edited by J. Bowring. (1962). New York: Russell & Russell.

Bentham, J. ([1776] 1969). "A Fragment on Government." In *A Bentham Reader*, edited by M. Mack. New York: Pegasus.

Berger, J. (1991, January 22). "'Africa-Centered' Proposal Outlined for a Trial School." *New York Times*, B3.

Bloom, A. (1987). *The Closing of the American Mind.* New York: Simon & Schuster.

Bowles, S., and Gintis, H. (1976). *Schooling in Capitalist America: Educational Reform and the Contradictions of Economic Life.* New York: Basic Books.

Boyer, E. L. (1992). Foreword to *School Choice,* Carnegie Foundation for the Advancement of Teaching. Princeton: Carnegie Foundation for the Advancement of Teaching.

Brandt, R. (1990/91a). "Conditions That Promote Excellence." *Educational Leadership* 48(4): 3.

Brandt, R. (1990/91b). "On Public Schools of Choice: Conversation with Seymour Fliegel." *Educational Leadership* 48(4): 20–25.

Bryk, A.; Easton, J.; Kerbow, D.; Rollow, S.; and Sebring, P. (1993). *A View from the Elementary Schools: The State of Reform in Chicago.* Chicago: Consortium on Chicago School Research.

Callahan, R. (1962). *Education and the Cult of Efficiency: A Study of the Social Forces That Have Shaped the Administration of the Public Schools.* Chicago: University of Chicago Press.

Carnegie Council on Adolescent Development. (1989). *Turning Points: Preparing American Youth for the 21st Century.* Washington, DC: Carnegie Corporation of New York.

Carnegie Foundation for the Advancement of Teaching. (1992). *School Choice.* Princeton: Carnegie Foundation for the Advancement of Teaching.

Carper, J. C., and Hunt, T. C. (1984). *Religious Schooling in America.* Birmingham, AL: Religious Education Press.

Chamberlin, D., Chamberlin, E., Drought, N., and Scott, W. (1942). *Adventure in American Education.* Vol. 4, *Did They Succeed in College? The Follow-up Study of the Graduates of the Thirty Schools.* New York: Harper.

Chapman, P. D. (1988). *Schools as Sorters: Lewis M. Terman, Applied Psychology, and the Intelligence Testing Movement, 1890–1930.* New York: New York University Press.

Chauncey, H. (1941). "Some Observations on Evaluation in the Eight-Year Study." *The North Central Association Quarterly,* 257–64.

Chubb, J., and Moe, T. (1990). *Politics, Markets, and America's Schools.* Washington, DC: Brookings Institute.

Chubb, J., and Moe, T. (1991). "Political Pollyannas." *Teachers College Record* 93(1): 161–65.

Cibulka, J. (1990). "Choice and the Restructuring of American Education." In *Choice in Education: Potential and Problems,* edited by W. L. Boyd and H. J. Walberg. Berkeley: McCutchan.

Cicourel, A., and Kitsuse, J. (1963). *The Educational Decision-Makers.* Indianapolis: Bobbs Merrill.

Clinton, W. (1994, January 26). "Excerpts from President Clinton's State of the Union Message." *New York Times,* A9.

Coleman, J. S. (1968). "The Concept of Equality of Educational Opportunity." *Harvard Educational Review* 38(1): 7–36.

Cookson, P. W. (1991). "Politics, Markets, and America's Schools: A Review." *Teachers College Record* 93(1): 156–60.

Coons, J., and Sugarman, S. (1978). *Education by Choice: The Case for Family Control*. Berkeley: University of California Press.

Cremin, L. A. (1961). *The Transformation of the School: Progressivism in American Education 1876–1957*. New York: Vintage Books.

Crosier, L. (1991). *Casualties of Privilege: Essays on Prep Schools' Hidden Culture*. Washington, DC: Avocus.

Cubberley, E. P. (1909). *Changing Conceptions of Education*. Boston: Houghton Mifflin.

Dalton Schools. (1942). In *Adventure in American Education*. Vol. 5, *Thirty Schools Tell Their Story: Each School Writes of Its Participation in the Eight-Year Study*. New York: Harper.

Danzberger, J. P.; Kirst, M. W.; and Usdan, M. D. (1992). *Governing Public Schools: New Times, New Requirements*. Washington, DC: Institute for Educational Leadership.

Delpit, L. (1988). "The Silenced Dialogue: Power and Pedagogy in Educating Other People's Children." *Harvard Educational Review* 58(3): 280–98.

Department of Education. (1991). *America 2000*. Washington, DC: Department of Education.

Department of the Interior. ([1918] 1928). *Cardinal Principles of Secondary Education*. Washington, DC: United States Government Printing Office.

De Witt, K. (1993, January 15). "Teachers Ask for Help in Fighting School Violence." *New York Times*, A8.

Dewey, J. ([1900] 1956). "The School and Society." In *The Child and the Curriculum and the School and Society*. Chicago: University of Chicago Press.

Dewey, J. (1915). *Schools of Tomorrow*. New York: Dutton.

Dewey, J. ([1916] 1966). *Democracy and Education*. New York: Free Press.

Dewey, J. (1922). "Human Nature and Conduct." In *John Dewey: The Middle Works, 1899–1924*, Vol. 14. Edited by J. A. Boydston. Carbondale and Edwardsville: Southern Illinois University Press.

Dewey, J. (1927). *The Public and Its Problems*. Athens, OH: Swallow Press.

Dewey, J. (1930). *Individualism Old and New*. New York: Minton, Balch.

Dewey, J. ([1938] 1963). *Experience and Education*. New York: Collier Macmillan.

Diederich, P. E. (1951). "The Eight-Year Study: More Comments." *School and Society* 73(1883): 41–42.

Eliot, C. W. ([1892] 1961). "Shortening and Enriching the Grammar School Course." In *Charles W. Eliot and Popular Education*, edited by E. Krug. New York: Bureau of Publications, Teachers College.

Eliot, C. W. ([1894] 1961). "Report of the Committee of Ten." In *Charles W. Eliot and Popular Education*, edited by E. Krug. New York: Bureau of Publications, Teachers College.

Eliot, C. W. ([1905] 1961). "The Fundamental Assumptions in the Report of the Committee of Ten." In *Charles W. Eliot and Popular Education*, edited by E. Krug. New York: Bureau of Publications, Teachers College.

Eliot, C. W. (1909). "Educational Reform and the Social Order." *The School Review* 17(4): 217–22.

Ellison, L. (1990/91). "The Many Facets of School Choice." *Educational Leadership* 48(4): 37.

Fantini, M. (1974). "Humanizing the Humanism Movement." *Phi Delta Kappan* 15(1): 400–402.

Farmer, R. (1984). "Humanistic Education and Self-Actualization Theory." *Education* 105(2): 162–72.

Featherstone, J. (1991). Foreword to *Progressive Education for the 1990s*, by K. Jervis and C. Montag. New York: Teachers College Press.

Feldhusen, J. (1989). "Synthesis of Research on Gifted Youth." *Educational Leadership* 46(6): 6–11.

Fiala, R., and Lanford, A. (1987). "Educational Ideology and the World Educational Revolution, 1950–1970." *Comparative Education Review* 31(3): 315–32.

Fine, B. (1942, February 8). "Assails Policies of Our Colleges on Admissions." *New York Times*, 5.

Finn, C. (1987). "The High School Dropout Problem." *Public Interest* 87: 3–22.

Finn, C. (1990). "Why We Need Choice." In *Choice in Education: Potential and Problems*, edited by W. L. Boyd and H. J. Walberg. Berkeley: McCutchan.

Fishman, A. (1987). "Literacy and Cultural Context: A Lesson from the Amish." *Language Arts* 64(8): 842–54.

Friedman, M. (1955). "The Role of Government in Education." In *Economics and the Public Interest*, edited by R. A. Solo. New Brunswick, NJ: Rutgers University Press.

Friedman, M., and Friedman, R. (1979). *Free to Choose*. New York: Avon.

Gardner, J. W. (1990). *Building Community*. Prepared for the Leadership Studies Program of Independent Sector.

Geller, L. (1982). "The Failure of Self-Actualization Theory: A Critique of Carl Rogers and Abraham Maslow." *Journal of Humanistic Psychology* 22(2): 56–73.

Giarelli, J., and Webb, R. (1980). "Higher Education, Meritocracy and Distributive Justice." *Educational Studies* 2: 221–38.

Giles, H. H., McCutchen, S. P., and Zechiel, A. N. (1942). *Adventure in American Education*. Vol. 2, *Exploring the Curriculum: The Work of the Thirty from the Viewpoint of Curriculum Consultants*. New York: Harper.

Glass, G., and Matthews, D. (1991). "Are Data Enough?" *Educational Researcher* 20(3): 24–27.

Goldberg, M. F. (1990/91). "Portrait of Deborah Meier." *Educational Leadership* 48(4): 26–28.

Goodlad, J. I. (1978, Jan./Feb.). "The Trouble with Humanistic Education." *Journal of Humanistic Education* II: 9–29.

Graham, P. (1984, Fall). "Schools: Cacophony About Practice, Silence About Purpose." *Daedalus* 113(4): 29–57.

Grant, G. (1988). *The World We Created at Hamilton High*. Cambridge, MA: Harvard University Press.

Gusfield, J. R. (1981). *The Culture of Public Problems: Drinking-Driving and the Symbolic Order.* Chicago: The University of Chicago Press.

Gutmann, A. (1982). "What's the Use of Going to School?" In *Utilitarianism and Beyond*, edited by A. Sen and B. Williams. Cambridge: Cambridge University Press.

Gutmann, A. (1985). "Communitarian Critics of Liberalism." *Philosophy and Public Affairs* 14(3): 308–22.

Gutmann, A. (1987). *Democratic Education.* Princeton: Princeton University Press.

Hacker, A. (1984, April 12). "The Schools Flunk Out." *New York Review of Books*, 35–40.

Hall, G. S. (1904). *Adolescence*, Vol. 2. New York: Appleton.

Hamilton, C. V. (1968). "Race and Education: A Search for Legitimacy." *Harvard Educational Review* 38(4): 669–84.

Hare, R. M. (1977). "Opportunity for What? Some Remarks on Current Disputes About Equality in Education." *Oxford Review of Education* 3(3): 207–16.

Hare, R. M. (1982). "Ethical Theory and Utilitarianism." In *Utilitarianism and Beyond*, edited by A. Sen and B. Williams. Cambridge: Cambridge University Press.

Hayek, F. (1976). *Law, Legislation, and Liberty.* Chicago: University of Chicago Press.

Henig, J. R. (1994). *Rethinking School Choice: Limits of the Market Metaphor.* Princeton: Princeton University Press.

Herbst, J. (1992). "The American People's College: The Lost Promise of Democracy in Education." *American Journal of Education* 100(3): 275–97.

Hillesheim, J. W. (1986). "Suffering and Self-Cultivation: The Case of Nietzsche." *Educational Theory* 36(2): 171–78.

Hirsch, E. D. (1987). *Cultural Literacy: What Every American Needs to Know.* Boston: Houghton Mifflin.

Hostetler, J. A. (1963). *Amish Society.* Baltimore: Johns Hopkins University Press.

Irwin, K. (1991). "The Eight Year Study." In *Progressive Education for the 1990s*, edited by K. Jervis and C. Montag. New York: Teachers College Press.

Johnson, H. G. (1946). "Weakness in the Eight-Year Study." *School and Society* 63(1642): 417–19.

Johnson, H. G. (1950). "Some Comments on the Eight-Year Study." *School and Society* 72(1875): 337–39.

Johnson, H. G. (1951). "Here We Go Again." *School and Society* 74(1909): 41–42.

Jones, K., and Williamson, K. (1979). "The Birth of the Schoolroom." *Ideology and Consciousness* 6: 59–110.

Kachel, D. (1989). "How the Amish Educate Their Children: Can We Learn from Them?" *Educational Horizons* 67(3): 93–97.

Kaufman-Osborn, T. V. (1985). "Pragmatism, Policy Science, and the State." *American Journal of Political Science* 29(4): 827–49.

Kearns, D. (1988). Quoted in "Xerox Chief Accuses Schools of Hurting the U.S. Economy." *New York Times*, October 27.

Kirp, D. (1982). *Just Schools: The Idea of Racial Equality in American Education*. Berkeley: University of California Press.

Kirst, M. (1984). *Who Controls Our Schools: American Values in Conflict*. New York: W. H. Freeman.

Kohlberg, L., and Mayer, R. (1972). "Development as the Aim of Education." *Harvard Educational Review* 42(4): 449–96.

Kohn, A. (1992). "Resistance to Cooperative Learning: Making Sense of Its Deletion and Dilution." *Journal of Education* 174: 38–56.

Kozol, J. ([1975] 1984). *The Night Is Dark and I Am Far from Home*. New York: Continuum.

Kozol, J. (1991). *Savage Inequalities*. New York: Crown.

Kraushaar, O. F. (1972). *American Nonpublic Schools: Patterns of Diversity*. Baltimore and London: Johns Hopkins University Press.

Kulik, C., and Kulik, J. (1982). "Effects of Ability Grouping on Secondary School Students: A Meta-analysis of Evaluation Findings." *American Educational Research Journal* 19(3): 415–28.

Lancelot, W. H. (1943). "A Close-up of the Eight-Year Study." *School and Society* 58(1511): 449–51.

Lancelot, W. H. (1945). "The Eight-Year Study Still Awaits Fair Appraisal." *School and Society,* 62(1610): 281–82.

Lasch, C. (1991). *The True and Only Heaven: Progress and Its Critics*. New York: Norton.

Lee, C. D., Lomotey, K., and Shujaa, M. (1990). "How Shall We Sing Our Sacred Song in a Strange Land? The Dilemma of Double Consciousness and the Complexities of an African-Centered Pedagogy." *Journal of Education* 172(2): 45–61.

Levin, H. M. (1990). "The Economics of Justice in Education." In *1990 Yearbook of the American Education Finance Association,* edited by D. Verstegen. Cambridge, MA: Ballinger.

Lindblom, C. (1959). "The Science of Muddling Through." *Public Administration* 19: 79–88.

Lindblom, C. E., and Cohen, D. K. (1979). *Usable Knowledge: Social Science and Social Problem Solving*. New Haven: Yale University Press.

Los Angeles Times. (1992, April 18). "Sword over the Public Schools." *Los Angeles Times*, B5.

Lyon, H. C. (1981). "Our Most Neglected Natural Resource." *Today's Education* 70(1): 15GS–20GS.

MacIntyre, A. (1981). *After Virtue*. Notre Dame: University of Notre Dame Press.

MacIntyre, A. (1991). "I'm Not a Communitarian, but . . . ." *The Responsive Community* 1(3): 91–92.

Mack, M. (1963). *Jeremy Bentham: An Odyssey of Ideas*. New York: Columbia University Press.

Mack, M. (1969). Introduction to *A Bentham Reader,* edited by M. Mack. New York: Pegasus.

Majone, G. (1980). "Policies as Theories." *Omega: The International Journal of Management Science* 8(2): 151–62.

Majone, G. (1989). *Evidence, Argument, and Persuasion in the Policy Process.* New Haven: Yale University Press.

Maslow, A. H. (1954). *Motivation and Personality.* New York: Harper & Row.

Maslow, A. H. (1968a). "Some Educational Implications of Humanistic Psychologies." *Harvard Educational Review* 38(4): 685–96.

Maslow, A. H. (1968b). "Music Education and Peak Experiences." *Music Educators Journal* 54: 72–75, 163–71.

Maslow, A. H. (1970). *Motivation and Personality.* New York: Harper & Row.

Maslow, A. H. (1979). "Humanistic Education." *Journal of Humanistic Psychology* 19(3): 13–27.

McCarty, H. (1983, April). "At the Edges of Perception: Humanistic Education in the '80s and Beyond." Paper presented at the annual meeting of the American Educational Research Association, Montreal.

McConn, M. (1942). Preface to *Adventure in American Education.* Vol. 4, *Did They Succeed in College? The Follow-up Study of the Graduates of the Thirty Schools,* by D. Chamberlin, E. Chamberlin, N. Drought, and W. Scott. New York: Harper.

McLaren, P. (1986). *Schooling as a Ritual Performance: Towards a Political Economy of Educational Symbols and Gestures.* London: Routledge & Kegan Paul.

McLaughlin, M., and Shields, P. (1987). "Involving Low-Income Parents in the Schools: A Role for Policy?" *Phi Delta Kappan* 69(2): 156–60.

McNeil, J. D. (1985). *Curriculum: A Comprehensive Introduction.* Boston: Little, Brown.

Meier, D. W. (1991, March 4). "Choice Can Save Public Education." *The Nation,* 266–71.

Metz, M. H. (1990). "Magnet Schools and the Reform of Public Schooling." In *Choice in Education: Potential and Problems,* edited by W. L. Boyd and H. J. Walberg. Berkeley: McCutchan.

Mill, J. S. ([1863] 1957). *Utilitarianism.* Edited by O. Piest. New York: Macmillan.

Moore, D., and Davenport, S. (1990). "Choice: The New Improved Sorting Machine." In *Choice in Education: Potential and Problems,* edited by W. L. Boyd and H. J. Walberg. Berkeley: McCutchan.

National Commission for Excellence in Education. (1983). *A Nation at Risk: The Imperative for Educational Reform.* Washington, DC: Department of Education.

National Governors' Association. (1986). *Time for Results: The Governors' 1991 Report on Education.* Washington, DC: National Governors' Association.

National Governors' Association. (1990). *Educating America for State Strategies for Achieving the National Education Goals.* Washington, DC: National Governors' Association.

New York Times. (1990, July 3). "Wrong Surgery for Sick Schools." *New York Times,* A16.

New York Times. (1991a, July 17). "Skimming the Cream Off Schools." *New York Times,* A20.

New York Times. (1991b, June 17). "What of the Children Left Behind?" *New York Times,* A14.

New York Times. (1993, April 12). "Preventing Violence at School." *New York Times,* A14.

Newmann, F. M., and Oliver, D. W. (1967). "Education and Community." *Harvard Educational Review* 37(1): 61–106.

Nicholls, J. G. (1989). *The Competitive Ethos and Democratic Education.* Cambridge, MA: Harvard University Press.

Noddings, N. (1984). *Caring: A Feminine Approach to Ethics and Moral Education.* Berkeley: University of California Press.

Noddings, N. (1992a). *The Challenge to Care in Schools: An Alternative Approach to Education.* New York: Teachers College Press.

Noddings, N. (1992b, March). "Excellence as a Guide to Educational Conversation." Presented at the annual meeting of the Philosophy of Education Society, Denver.

Nozick, R. (1974). *Anarchy, State, and Utopia.* New York: Basic Books.

Oakes, J. (1985). *Keeping Track: How Schools Structure Inequality.* New Haven: Yale University Press.

Oakes, J. (1986a). "Keeping Track. Part 1. The Policy and Practice of Curriculum Inequality." *Phi Delta Kappan* 68(1): 12–17.

Oakes, J. (1986b). "Tracking, Inequality, and the Rhetoric of Reform: Why Schools Don't Change." *Journal of Education* 168(1): 60–80.

Oakes, J. (1992). "Can Tracking Research Inform Practice? Technical, Normative, and Political Considerations." *Educational Researcher* 21(4): 12–21.

Oakes, J., Selvin, M., Karoly, L., and Guiton, G. (1992). *Educational Matchmaking: Academic and Vocational Tracking in Comprehensive High Schools.* Santa Monica, CA: Rand.

Oakes, J., and Sirotnik, K. A. (1983). "An Immodest Proposal: From Critical Theory to Critical Practice for School Renewal." (Monograph). Los Angeles: University of California, Laboratory in School and Community Education and Center for the Study of Evaluation.

Okin, S. M. (1979). *Women in Western Political Thought.* Princeton: Princeton University Press.

Oliver, R. G. (1982). "Rousseau's *Émile* and Its Contribution to the Development of Educational Theory." *Teachers College Record* 84(2): 493–508.

Perko, F. M., ed. (1988). *Enlightening the Next Generation: Catholics and Their Schools 1830–1980.* New York and London: Garland.

Peterson, J. M. (1989). "Tracking Students by Their Supposed Abilities Can Derail Learning." *The American School Board Journal* 176(5): 38.

Pitkin, H. F. (1990). "Slippery Bentham: Some Neglected Cracks in the Foundations of Utilitarianism." *Political Theory* 18(1): 104–31.

Plato. (trans. 1955). *The Republic.* Harmondsworth, England: Penguin Books.

Power, F. C., Higgins, A., and Kohlberg, L. (1989). *Lawrence Kohlberg's Approach to Moral Education.* New York: Columbia University Press.

Preskill, S. (1989). "Educating for Democracy: Charles W. Eliot and the Differentiated Curriculum." *Educational Theory* 39(4): 351–58.

Progressive Education Association. (1930). "Principles." *Progressive Education* 1:1.

Purkey, S., and Smith, M. (1983). "Effective Schools: A Review." *The Elementary School Journal* 83(4): 427–52.

Ravitch, D. (1985). *The Schools We Deserve: Reflections on the Educational Crises of Our Time.* New York: Basic Books.

Rawls, J. (1971). *A Theory of Justice.* Cambridge, MA: Harvard University Press.

Raywid, M. A. (1985). "Family Choice Arrangements in Public Schools: A Review of the Literature." *Review of Educational Research* 55(4): 435–67.

Raywid, M. A. (1987). "Public Choice, Yes; Vouchers, No!" *Phi Delta Kappan* 68(10): 762–69.

Redefer, F. L. (1950). "The Eight Year Study . . . After Eight Years." *Progressive Education* 28(2): 33–36.

Rehberg, R. A., and Rosenthal, E. R. (1978). *Class and Merit in the American High School.* New York: Longman.

Responsive Communitarian Platform: Rights and Responsibilities. (1991/92). *The Responsive Community* 2: 4–20.

Ritter, A. G., and Bondanella, J. C., eds. (1988). *Rousseau's Political Writings.* New York: Norton.

Roemer, J. (1988). *Free to Lose: An Introduction to Marxist Economic Philosophy.* Cambridge, MA: Harvard University Press.

Rogers, C. (1977, Jan./Feb.). "The Politics of Education." *Journal of Humanistic Education,* 6–22.

Rogers, C. (1983). *Freedom to Learn for the 80's.* Columbus, OH: Merrill.

Rorty, R. (1989, July). "The Opening of American Minds." *Harper's Magazine,* 18–22.

Rosenbaum, J. (1976). *Making Inequality: The Hidden Curriculum of High School Tracking.* New York: Wiley.

Rosenbaum, J. (1980). "Social Implications of Educational Grouping." *Review of Research in Education,* 361–401.

Rosenberg, B. (1990/91). "Not a Case for Market Control." *Educational Leadership* 48(4): 64–65.

Rosenow, E. (1989). "Nietzsche's Educational Dynamite." *Educational Theory* 39(4): 307–16.

Rousseau, J. J. ([1762] 1956). *The Émile of Jean Jacques Rousseau.* Translated and edited by W. Boyd. New York: Teachers College Press.

Rousseau, J. J. ([1762, 1755] 1967). *The Social Contract and Discourse on the Origin of Inequality.* Edited by L. G. Crocker. New York: Simon & Schuster.

Sandel, M. (1982). *Liberalism and the Limits of Justice.* Cambridge: Cambridge University Press.

Sapon-Shevin, M., and Schniedewind, N. (1992). "If Cooperative Learning's the Answer, What Are the Questions?" *Journal of Education* 174: 11–37.

Sautter, R. C. (1978). "The Four Billion Dollar Lunch." *Instructor* 88(2): 46–51.

Scheffler, I. (1984). "On the Education of Policymakers." *Harvard Educational Review* 54(2): 152–65.

Scheffler, I. (1985). *On Human Potential.* Boston: Routledge & Kegan Paul.

Schneider, J. (1989). "Tracking: A National Perspective." *Equity and Choice* 6(1): 11–22.

Sen, A., and Williams, B., eds. (1982). *Utilitarianism and Beyond.* Cambridge: Cambridge University Press.

Shannon, T. (1990/91). "Less Government Is Not the Answer." *Educational Leadership* 48(4): 61–62.

Sharan, S. (1980). "Cooperative Learning in Small Groups: Recent Methods and Effects on Achievement, Attitudes, and Ethnic Relations." *Review of Educational Research* 50(2): 241–71.

Sheviakov, G. V., and Block, J. F. (1942). "Evaluation of Personal and Social Adjustment." In *Adventure in American Education,* Vol. 3, *Appraising and Recording Student Progress: Evaluation, Records and Reports in Thirty Schools,* edited by E. R. Smith and R. W. Tyler. New York: Harper.

Silberman, C. E. (1971). *Crisis in the Classroom: The Remaking of American Education.* New York: Vintage Books.

Slavin, R. E. (1987). "Ability Grouping and Its Alternative: Must We Track?" *American Educator,* 32–48.

Slavin, R. E. (1990). "Achievement Effects of Ability Grouping in Secondary Schools: A Best-Evidence Synthesis." *Review of Educational Research* 60(3): 471–99.

Slavin, R. E. (1991). "Are Cooperative Learning and 'Untracking' Harmful to the Gifted?" *Educational Leadership* 48(6): 68–71.

Smart, J. J. C., and Williams, B. (1973). *Utilitarianism: For and Against.* Cambridge: Cambridge University Press.

Smith, E. R., and Tyler, R. W., eds. (1942). *Adventure in American Education.* Vol. 3, *Appraising and Recording Student Progress: Evaluation, Records and Reports in Thirty Schools.* New York: Harper.

Smith, M. B. (1969). *Social Psychology and Human Values.* Chicago: Aldine.

Smith, M. B. (1973). "On Self-Actualization: A Trans-ambivalent Examination of a Focal Theme in Maslow's Psychology." *Journal of Humanistic Psychology* 13(2): 17–33.

Smith, M. B. (1990). "Humanistic Psychology." *Journal of Humanistic Psychology* 30(4): 6–21.

Strike, K. A. (1991). "The Moral Role of Schooling in a Liberal Democratic Society." In *Review of Research in Education,* Vol. 17. Edited by G. Grant. Washington, DC: American Educational Research Association.

Strike, K. A. (1989). *Liberal Justice and the Marxist Critique of Education: A Study of Conflicting Research Programs.* New York: Routledge, Chapman, & Hall.

Swidler, A. (1982). "The Culture of Policy: Aggregate Versus Individualist Thinking About the Regulation of Education." Project Report No. 82-A13 prepared for the IFG Seminar on Law and Governance, CERAS, Stanford University.

Taba, H., and McGuire, C. (1942). "Evaluation of Social Sensitivity." In *Adventure in American Education.* Vol. 3, *Appraising and Recording Student Progress: Evaluation, Records and Reports in Thirty Schools,* edited by E. R. Smith and R. W. Tyler. New York: Harper.

Terman, L. (1920). "The Use of Intelligence Tests in the Grading of School Children." *Journal of Educational Research* 1(1): 20–32.

Thirty Schools. (1942). In *Adventure in American Education*. Vol. 5, *Thirty Schools Tell Their Story: Each School Writes of Its Participation in the Eight-Year Study*. New York: Harper.

Tocqueville, A. de ([1848] 1966). *Democracy in America*. Translated by G. Lawrence and edited by J. P. Mayer. New York: Harper & Row.

Tozer, S., Violas, P., and Senese, G. (1993). *School & Society: Educational Practice as Social Expression*. New York: McGraw-Hill.

Tucker, A. M., and Lauber, W. F., eds. (1994). *School Choice Programs: What's Happening in the States*. Washington, DC: Heritage Foundation.

Tulsa High Schools. (1942). In *Adventure in American Education*. Vol. 5, *Thirty Schools Tell Their Story: Each School Writes of Its Participation in the Eight-Year Study*. New York: Harper.

Turney, A. H. (1931). "The Status of Ability Grouping." *Educational Administration and Supervision* 17: 21–42, 110–27.

Tweedie, J. (1990). "Should Market Forces Control Educational Decision Making?" *American Political Science Review* 84(2): 549–54.

Twentieth Century Fund. (1983). *Making the Grade: Report of the Task Force on Federal Elementary and Secondary Education Policy*. New York: Twentieth Century Fund.

Tyack, D. (1974). *The One Best System*. Cambridge, MA: Harvard University Press.

Tyack, D., and Hansot, E. (1981, Summer). "Conflict and Consensus in American Public Education," *Daedalus* 110(3): 1–25.

Tyack, D., and Hansot, E. (1982). *Managers of Virtue: Public School Leadership in America, 1820–1980*. New York: Basic Books.

Tyack, D., and Hansot, E. (1988). "Silence and Policy Talk: Historical Puzzles About Gender and Education." *Educational Researcher* 17(3): 33–41.

Tyler, R. W. (1944). "A Comment on Professor Lancelot's Criticism of the 'Eight-Year' Study." *School and Society* 59(1536): 396.

Tyler, R. W. (1980). "What Was Learned from the Eight-Year Study." *New York University Education Quarterly* 11(2): 29–32.

Tyler, R. W. (1986/87). "The Five Most Significant Curriculum Events in the Twentieth Century." *Educational Leadership* 44(4): 36–38.

Underhill, A. (1989). "Process in Humanistic Education." *ELT Journal* 43(4): 250–60.

University School, Ohio State University. (1942). In *Adventure in American Education*. Vol. 5, *Thirty Schools Tell Their Story: Each School Writes of Its Participation in the Eight-Year Study*. New York: Harper.

Useem, E. (1990, April). "Social Class and Ability Group Placement in Mathematics in the Transition to Seventh Grade: The Role of Parent Involvement." Paper presented at the annual meeting of the American Educational Research Association, Boston.

Wall Street Journal. (1990, March 29). "Up From Mediocrity." *Wall Street Journal*, A12.

Walzer, M. (1983). *Spheres of Justice*. New York: Basic Books.

Weiss, C. (1980). *Social Science Research and Decision-Making*. New York: Columbia University Press.

Wells, A. S. (1991). "Choice in Education: Examining the Evidence on Equity." *Teachers College Record* 93(1): 137–55.

Wells, A. S. (1993). *Time to Choose: America at the Crossroads of School Choice Policy*. New York: Hill & Wang.

Westbrook, R. (1991). *John Dewey and American Democracy*. Ithaca, NY: Cornell University Press.

Westbrook, R. (1992). "Schools for Industrial Democrats: The Social Origins of John Dewey's Philosophy of Education." *American Journal of Education* 100(4): 401–19.

Wigginton, E. (1986). *Sometimes a Shining Moment: The Foxfire Experience*. Garden City, NY: Anchor Press/Doubleday Books.

Wildavsky, A. (1987). *Speaking Truth to Power: The Art and Craft of Policy Analysis*. New Brunswick, NJ: Transaction Books.

Index

About the Author

Joseph Kahne is an assistant professor of policy studies in the College of Education of the University of Illinois at Chicago and the codirector of the Chicago Network for Service Learning and Democratic Citizenship. He received his doctorate in education from Stanford University and has published a number of scholarly journal articles on educational policy analysis and school reform. This is his first book.